# Enough.

# Enough.

## Discover Your Unique Worth
## and Live Your God-Given Purpose

Dr Kathrine McAleese

A CIP catalogue record for this book is available from the
British Library

ISBN 978-1-7391675-0-9 (paperback)
ISBN 978-1-7391675-1-6 (ebook)

Edited by Erin Chamberlain
Cover design by Kristen Ingebretson
Typeset by Su Richards
Proofread by Mary Davis

For Ronnie and Laura.

I am forever grateful that God gave me you two as my parents.

This is for and because of you.

# Contents

# Introduction

THIS book is for you if you've ever doubted yourself, wondered what was wrong with you, or felt like you just maybe weren't up to the task because what seems so easy to others feels like wading through treacle for you. If you know what it is to feel overwhelmed or burned out, or felt like a freak because how you're 'supposed' to show up feels alien to you, then this book is going to be balm for your weary soul.

I know this because I've been helping women for over 25 years to set goals that they're actually excited to achieve, then, crucially, helping them develop the mindset required to fulfil and exceed those goals. I have achieved that in multiple domains – whether helping dancers to successfully audition for professional theatre school, or gain their dance teaching qualification, and through my two current businesses. In one of these businesses, I help dog sport competitors with their mindset from novices up to those wanting to achieve goals at national and world levels. My other business is where I help women to tweak their existing business so that it better fits the pace of life that lights them up. In short, I help these women be who they were put here to be, at an un-hustled, God-designed pace.

You might not think that these relate to each other, or are relevant to you, but humans are humans, and the 'gremlins' that sabotage your thinking are really no different than those that sabotage women building their dream businesses, or those stepping up to the start line at a national or world championships.

This book is designed to help you begin that journey for yourself, whether you have competitive goals, want to pace yourself better as you move forward in your own business, or are just fed up with how you currently feel about yourself.

I'm predominantly going to speak from the perspective of having your own business, but even if you've never had, nor ever want to have, your own business, you're going to find lively stories packed with universal truths wrapped up in them, regardless of where this finds you in life. No matter how you came to be reading this, know that you are precious beyond measure – whether you currently believe that or not. I don't believe that it is an accident that you are reading this at this moment in time, so I pray and anticipate that there will be juicy AHAs in this book for you. You matter, you have purpose and I trust that you'll leave this book with a stronger sense of those facts.

# 1:

## Dance like only dog walkers are watching

WHEN I was a child, I danced all the time. I'd dance in our front room and, as it got dark, the windows would become mirrors and I could see my creations come to life in the reflection. Including the imperfections. I'd repeat and practise, constantly choreographing improvised routines to whatever music fed my soul in that moment. Goodness knows what people walking up the street thought, but I simply didn't care, I was lost in what I was doing. This was back before the age of the Internet, when dog walkers were my only potential audience!

These days, it's a different proposition to allow yourself to be seen, since it's not just neighbours and passing dog walkers who see you, but an entire online world. Images and posts can be immortalised in a screenshot. You can be exposed to a slew of opinions, and those opinions can be vomited out in the comments, from people you've never met. People who will never get – nor take – time to truly know and understand you beyond the instant judgement they've made from the snapshot you shared. Is it any wonder that you start second-guessing what you should share, in a valid attempt at self-preservation! Think of this fear as a weed that sucks nutrition from your life's soil, if allowed to grow.

That conditioning and training in how you 'should' be and what you should project to the world starts much earlier than adulthood though, and the lessons you learn about yourself are often forming you long before you try to put yourself out there to build that business you dream of or pursue that competitive goal. Some of this social learning is good and necessary for us to grow into functioning and contributing members of society, rather than selfish leeches who suck the life out of each other. The flip side though is that some aspects of social training can invite you to shut down your dreams and the unique contribution you could have in the world by placing labels on you that set limits for you specifically, or 'someone like you' more generally. For example, the common wisdom in online business is to share personal stories and snapshots from your life on a regular, ongoing basis. Perhaps even be doing regular live videos to really work the current algorithms' whims. You're not a freak to wonder if there's something wrong with you when you don't want to share your whole life online. Perhaps you've been told that you need to be more visible in a bunch of online groups to be seen and form connections. There's nothing wrong with either of these things, *per se*, but if you're not wired that way, you are not deficient if you find the idea of speaking up in 'communities' of thousands online to be hellish.

At the risk of repeating the punchline, the whole point of this book is that you were not wired to be some cookie-cutter clone of anyone else. You are different, and you will have impact differently, because you are wired to be YOU, and YOU alone. You were created because your world needed YOU to be you, not an imposter trying to be someone else. I know that's a pretty heady idea, but before it strikes you as megalomaniacal, let me explain a little more of where we are actually going with this!

## Let me introduce you to yourself

*'Is this it?'*
*'What's wrong with me?'*
*'Why does it seem much easier for others?'*

If any of this sounds familiar, then you are in the right place. This book is for you. If you're like many of my clients, you've already been working on improving yourself and you've probably taken the time to learn all the strategies and skills that are supposed to make you successful. Maybe this is your first step in personal development rather than skills-specific training, and you're reading this because it's all feeling stressful and overwhelming. You have achieved a lot already, you know that. And yet, it's EXHAUSTING. Burnout and overwhelm are familiar and, although you're experiencing some success, honestly it feels like wading through treacle in a tutu. You wonder sometimes if you've got what it takes when others seem to find it so easy. You wonder if you're not cut out for greater success... I mean, if you were, surely it would have happened by now? Honestly, you're tired of feeling like you're not enough, and on your worst days, feeling like a freak.

## You matter

Let's get something straight from the get-go. I don't care what you've ever been told: you are not an accident. Your parents may have been accidental parents, but no matter what anyone told you, you are not an accident. This might seem like a funny place to start, but I'm a straight-no-chaser kind of person who values authenticity. I know that we will disagree on some things. Since I am not you, OF COURSE we will. I'm fine with that and I hope you are too.

**BIG** IDEA: You matter, you have purpose, and you are meant to be here at this time. You're unique by design, that is intentional and the unique cocktail of expertise and experience that makes you *you* is not merely 'enough', but inherently priceless. You are YOU, not a knock-off of someone else, so it's time for you to meet and be her.

That's why, from the outset, I want you to understand where I'm coming from so that you can see where we agree, and where we don't.

Everyone has a worldview and mine is shaped by being a Jesus-following woman. DON'T STOP READING! Look, *I know* the term 'Christian' is toxic for many because of how some have co-opted it to justify truly awful things. I do NOT condone those. I also don't need you to agree with me. Many of my clients don't share my worldview so I don't expect you to either. Your worldview is *your* homework to work out, not mine, so if you want to take the faith stuff with a pinch of salt and treat this as an academic exercise to spur creative thought, then go for it! It's my faith that drives me to tell you from the outset that YOU MATTER. Your parents may not have intended you, but God did.

You were dreamt up in love, designed with delight by God who fiercely loves you and craves relationship with you. You are worth everything to Him. I wholeheartedly believe that you were created with purpose and that your gifts and talents were God-given, to benefit you, and through you, to benefit others. That doesn't mean everyone needs to have some dramatic role in the world – your role may be to bake cakes for housebound neighbours – and I have full faith that you can have a bigger impact[1] with that kindness and presence than many seven-figure entrepreneurs. Don't make the mistake of imagining that you have to do something 'big' to make a difference. The 'small' things are only deemed that by others who haven't felt the benefit of them. To the recipient of the 'small' kindnesses, you may make the world of difference, even if you never know that this side of eternity. God believes in you and purposed you to be here on earth at this moment in history, and for whatever reason, to be reading this book.

## How this book works

As we go through these chapters and exercises, we're going to explore who you're currently being, who you have been in different contexts in the past and who you were created to be – who you **can** be in future.

As we explore, you're going to begin to recognise the conditioning and labels that you've been given on your journey through your life. You'll be able to see where those labels and conditioning are constricting you and holding you back. Then you will be able to begin the work of stepping freely into the fullness of who you were put here to be, and to have the impact on the world you were created to have.

I danced without a care as a child, but this book comes after many years of being far more conscious of what others see. I spent far too long learning how to show up in my online business, learning the skills and tactics, all the strategies and messaging I simply must know and use... and look, there is a place for technique, but it's not enough alone. My dancing certainly needed all the help it could get on the technique front as I was far more 'artist' than 'technician' – but when that artistry was aided by technique, I came into my own and was able to give my best.

That's the point though, it's not either/or, it's both/and. Artistry and technique. This book is about unleashing the artistry of who you are, and who you were created to be, into a world that too often tries to distil success into a one-size-fits-all formula, a neat system with a clear number of steps. Although that can certainly work for some, I want to pose a nuanced perspective on what 'success' might look like for you and how your 'impact' may be far deeper and more profound than anything that can be measured by financial metrics alone, no matter how lovely those metrics can be.

My background is in performing arts, then a degree in theology, before becoming a qualified marriage and family therapist and later refining my skills further as a sociologist. I've been self-employed for over 25 years and have spent well over a decade of that working in the online space – teaching, coaching and mentoring clients through live seminars, online classes and my podcasts. You can find out more about all of these at **www.drkathrine.com**. I also offer 1–1 services to selected clients, run a high-level small group Mastermind, and host boutique retreats – helping female coaches and service-based business owners to live and work at an un-hustled, God-designed pace which is uniquely suited to them.

> **If she can, you can**
>
> **ACPAT** Physiotherapist Gillian Barrett says: 'I was brought up to do things for other people and if I needed something to try to do it myself. Kat has helped me learn to set better boundaries, making time to work on the business as well as in it and making time for myself as well. I've also gained confidence to put myself out in public more – a podcast interview, monthly newsletter to clients and working on a couple of short ebooks.'

I've split this book into three parts, and each chapter is designed so you can get in and out quickly with what you need to have epiphanies and make any changes you want to. The three parts are split into the different parts of your life story landscape:

- Who you are
- Who you were
- Who you were created to be

We're going to start in Part 1 with who you currently believe you are. This is where we identify the 'fruits' that have got you this far and that you'll want to keep, nurture, prune and strengthen for the future... not to mention the 'weeds' that need to be pulled up and removed from your life's metaphorical garden, so that other things can be planted, grow and thrive instead. This is a great opportunity to give yourself credit for what you're already doing well, as well as root out the rotten fruit and weeds that are just a pain to deal with. Just as you wouldn't shame yourself for a weed growing in your garden (at least I hope you wouldn't – weeds happen!), I hope you'll start the way you mean to go on and give yourself a lot of grace. You've been through a lot to get this far – both good and bad – so let's walk through this together with a hefty dose of gentleness to yourself, OK?

I've started with the present rather than the past because it really is easier to see the fruit than the root, so we'll start with what we can see around us, and work down and up from there.

You may want to skip this bit and get to the sexy stuff, to the future where everything is epic. It's your life so you can do what you want, but I encourage you to access whatever stubborn-as-a-mule grit you have in you and show Part 1 who is boss. Every time that little whisper wants you to think 'I know this' or roll your eyes at something because you think you know where I'm going with a topic, I invite you to consider that you've not read it in this context before. If you've done a lot of personal development work, you're not the same person who heard it before. Just like changing seasons alter the view over the landscape around you, so the connections your brain makes this time around, and the AHAs it may serve up are likely to be different than in the past. I dare you to treat even the seemingly familiar as an exploration of what your mind wants to highlight for you, and approach it with expectancy! The future is coming, you don't need to force it.

In Part 2, we turn to the past. You didn't become the 'you' you are today in a vacuum. There are forces beyond yourself that have honed and shaped you, that have corralled and limited you, that have lifted you and carried you. You weren't created in a bubble, and you don't live a sterile life devoid of human contact on a desert island somewhere. You are part of a wider world, connected to the people around you locally, with ripples that reach out to global connections. There are factors that impact who you are and how you learned to navigate this world that are not your within your control. Factors such as prejudice and discriminatory barriers are put in some people's way whilst others are never subjected to them, whether those barriers are on the basis of sex, race, religion, and so on. Throughout this book I will be helping you connect yourself and your experience to others.

This is powerful because if you've been walking through life as if you are a walking collection of irredeemable failures, you may find that shame feels like a constant companion. When you understand that you are impacted by factors beyond yourself, and can better recognise those influences on you, it helps you to better work out where you need to give your head a wobble, and where the credit actually belongs somewhere else entirely. There are specific challenges that have been put in your path that differ from those of others. That means the journey you take will be different from others. That doesn't excuse you to shrug and quit! It *does* encourage you to navigate the real world you live in, not some idealised one of seven simple steps that your quintessential white male guru laid down as being the secret to his success. They may very well be part of the secret to his success, and I congratulate him, but your situation, responsibilities and resources may not be the same, so understanding what is different for you will help you ignore the messages that don't apply so you can focus on what actually will help YOU.

This is crucial, because too many of the women I work with have been shamed for being who they are, by the very same culture that has limited, shamed and trained them into the very (small) version of themselves they now are. This is at best ignorant, at worst disingenuous, and either way, it is harmful. Once you understand the context that the current 'you' developed in, you can get rid of a lot of shame and can make different choices, because your understanding of who you have been in the middle of all that is changed.

That's why in Part 2 we're going to look back at remembering who you were, the context you were in, and develop a richer story of who you have been, in light of this new contextual knowledge. There is immense power in understanding the broader context in which you have learned and grown up, and it can truly shift unhelpful stories that have been stuck for years, if not decades. Bearing witness to the different perspectives you can take on a situation, and having others bear witness for you, offers ways to comprehend your experiences differently. You can understand them as the woman you are now, with the benefit of difference and hearing others' input, even if you decide to reject their input as wrong or inappropriate because they do not know everything that you know about the situation. Don't get bogged down in this: it's simply to acknowledge people who have informed your thinking, and to accept that none of us are 'self-made'. We are all crafted in the ebb and flow, the interplay and clashes between ourselves and others, both directly and indirectly. And that dynamic is not just in this moment in time, but echoes with the ripples of eternity too. This part will also give you space to recognise the people, places, influences and experiences that strengthened you, that helped you to get to where you are, that kept you going and inspired you.

## Two things to note about Part 2

Firstly, this is not about blaming everything on your childhood. We're not going there and, at all times, you choose how closely – or not – you want to look back at any area of your life. This is not therapy and as such, I am going to particularly focus on societal aspects since those are often more subtle, overlooked, and insidious.

Secondly, this section does not absolve you of responsibility going forward. This is not a 'my culture made me do it' exercise. Rather, once you know better, the responsibility is absolutely yours to do something with what you know, to use it to inform you for the future.

Finally, in Part 3, we're going to look to the future, armed with a fresh perspective on who you've been up until this moment and who you can become, so it will be time to let go and really dream. Knowing what makes your soul sing, and knowing what you've dreamt in the past, how do you want to proceed? Where can you make a difference? What does that look like for *you*? What did God put in you that resistance and fear have kept you from sharing with the world? What would the enemy of your soul be really happy for you to keep hidden? My hope for this section is that this will inspire you and light a fire under you to go forth and be fully, gloriously, you in the world, equipped to sidestep many more of the pitfalls than you've ever been ready to before. Time is marching on, and we're all hurtling towards eternity, so let's get on with it!

# PART 1: Who are you?

# 2:

## Words have power

THERE'S an ancient wisdom that says 'the tongue has the power of life and death'.[2] If you've ever worked with me, particularly if you've ever worked with me in person, you can pretty much bet that I will start with the power of words. Think about their power this way: you cannot describe yourself without words. Try it. Look in the mirror and describe what you see without using words. It's impossible. Try it!

At some level you already know that words have power: whether it's someone telling you that they don't love you anymore, or a teacher who inspired your studies with repeated encouragement and well-placed redirection, we can all point to words that have been spoken over us at various points, whether good words or bad – they made an impression. Some of them left a mark.

The words we hear about, and over, ourselves are not the only ones we hear. You've heard the words, insults and accusations thrown at someone who transgressed a group's norms. What was said about them? Words. Those words that weren't spoken over you may nevertheless have impacted how you act today, or who you believe you are today.

There are also the words that you speak to yourself. Those words you use to and about yourself so often you don't even notice yourself saying them anymore. 'I'm so stupid', 'I'm really clumsy', 'I'm so forgetful' or 'I'm an excellent coach', 'I'm a powerful speaker', 'I have great insights that many people clamour to listen to'. If those latter phrases felt awkward or arrogant, don't worry, we'll get to that shortly. As you read, pay attention to the words you are using to and about yourself. Are you your best cheerleader, your own worst enemy or a combination of the two? I *know* you will be tempted to skip the questions or tell yourself that you'll come back to them, but let's be honest, you really won't, so even just take 30 seconds on each and see how it pays off by the time we're done. This is a reader participation book because you are far more expert on your life than I can ever hope to be.

More than that, this is your life and it's up to you to direct it, not sit on the sidelines and hope that someone else stunt doubles for you.

Every time you come to a section with an 'Over to You' and a bunch of questions, I dare you to slow down enough to write down what comes to mind as you work through the questions. When you do this, you will not just be getting the most from what I share, because by taking time to answer them as we go along, whether they're in the middle of a chapter or at the end, you will be bringing your mind to collaborate with mine. The connections that your mind makes as you put it to work will lead to epiphanies that I could never predict, because you, your knowledge and your experiences are unique, so what you can get from this book when we work together is also going to be unique. You are always free to gloss over questions if there are ones you don't want to ponder, but don't miss out on our time together by simply ignoring the questions or telling yourself you'll come back to them later.

## Stories

Your life is a series of stories, told and recalled in words. Sometimes the very thought of them brings attachments of shame, so to help with that, I'm going to use playful stories and analogies that create a different way of looking at yourself and your life, to allow room for new perspectives and fresh information to break through the old well-rehearsed stories you've been telling yourself about who you are.

Let's start with a garden analogy. Let's use that playful analogy to take a step back and think about the various types of stories you have in your memory. Picture your life now as a garden and imagine each story is a plant in that garden. This garden is full of fruit and vegetables, some nuts and yes, some weeds. There's probably a few plants that you don't know the identity of too. Each one of those plants represents a story from your life. Some of them are huge trees spanning decades like the stories they represent. Those stories have been with you all or much of your life. Others are thin, spindly shoots, telling the story of a fleeting moment or experience. Some of the plants are well used. You've eaten their crops repeatedly and have all sorts of understanding of what makes them grow. They have some damaged leaves, but some of these plants are your most cherished.

Some of the well-picked fruit plants may also be the most painful. Their pain doesn't come from the number of crops you've had out of them, but rather their thorns – what those metaphorical thorns depict, what they remind you of, or who said the words that made this plant such a thorny one. Some of the plants in your life's garden may need professional help. Those stories that have deeply wounded you may be best brought out in therapy to help you tame them or uproot them so they have less ability to hurt you, and that can be a daunting task that is made far easier when you're not trying to do it alone.

Other plants might not need professional assistance to deal with, but they may be ones you'll want to uproot or clip into shape because you don't like them anymore or they simply no longer serve you. An expert perspective on those plants will help you to prune them correctly and really get the best out of them because the specialists looking at them will not just see symptoms, but are trained to recognise what is causing the symptoms, and can help you effectively support the plant's development and changing needs as it grows.

Some of the plants are going to look different by the time we're done because you'll be looking at yourself and your life from a different perspective that gives a fuller account of what got planted in the past, what is growing now and what you want it all to look like in future.

The thing about some plants is that the difference between them is one of perception under the gaze of the garden owner, as well as subject to their priorities and the particular placement of the particular plant. A plant may look like a weed to one person, either because it's not what they think of as valuable (perception), or because it has taken root where it was not wanted (placement). Maybe they don't recognise that its existence is actually valuable to their ultimate goal (priorities). To another person, or from a different perspective, that weed is a valued wildflower that feeds bees or attracts butterflies or is a rare find.

Whichever plant any experience in your life resembles, if you were to try to describe them, you would use words to do so. The words you choose matter, because words have meaning and that meaning influences what you feel and what you do in light of those thoughts and feelings. Just as with the weed/wildflower example, it's not a matter of being 'wrong' but of perception, priorities and placement.

To help you grasp the power of words, I want to tell you about a story that one of my clients held about herself.

Sally[3] felt like she couldn't focus long enough to complete a round of competition with her dog in agility. She felt like her focus was constantly going all over the place and she was frustrated, feeling that she couldn't stay focused on the course she was supposed to be guiding her dog round, which kept resulting in faults and eliminations. We talked about what was happening, and I was curious about what Sally did in the rest of life, when she wasn't competing, for example, in her work. Sally told me that she teaches a class of children with additional educational needs. In the course of that work, she must constantly be vigilant in case trouble is brewing or a child is doing anything that could be dangerous.

Now, imagine that's how your brain has been honed. You have spent decades developing your superpower for keeping children safe and engaged as a teacher. You, by necessity, would have developed what we call over here a set of 'eyes like a travelling rat', meaning you are able to take in all kinds of stimuli and process it for extended periods of time.

Is it any wonder that your superpower is still switched on when you come to compete! From a different perspective, the same skills that allowed her to actually educate the children in the midst of the stimuli are the very skills she could recruit to compete in competition.

This gave Sally a whole new way of looking at what she was experiencing. She wasn't a 'failure', 'getting old', 'lacking focus' or 'not up to it'. She was someone with a superpower that could be dialled down whilst another *existing* superpower was recruited and dialled up in this context. She knew she could do this, because she had decades of experience of using her skills in exactly that way, just in a different context. She didn't *lack* the skill she needed, she just needed to recognise the skills she had, and generalise her behaviour so that she was using those skills in the context of competition!

Imagine how Sally felt, realising that she'd not been using these bigger picture skills that she draws on daily, nor giving herself credit for something which she'd been perceiving as a weakness!

What would it be like for you to look with fresh eyes at what you're experiencing and see your obstacles with the aid of existing strengths you'd not even noticed you had?

### I am...

As promised, here are a bunch of questions as the reader participation section of the book begins! Grab a pen and a piece of paper. DON'T READ AHEAD. Use good old-fashioned pen and paper, so you can see it in your writing.

Have you got your pen and paper ready? OK. Once you've read what I'm going to ask of you, I want you to scribble down the first things that come into your head, as quickly as you can. Don't allow yourself time to analyse or question, just write.

Pen at the ready? Over to you!

---

### OVER TO YOU

Write down the first five words that come to mind to describe YOU. Don't think, just write. Go!

- What did you write?
- Do you like what you wrote?

- Were they words that built you up or tore you down? A mixture?
- How do these words feel in your body to read? Take a moment with each word individually and think about the images that come to mind – the memories, stories, people, who you associate with that word relating to you.
- How old are these words? Are they ones you've only started to attribute to yourself recently or are they words with a long history with you?

---

The reason this is so important is that who you believe you are, and where you derive your sense of value from will always leak out in how you behave. This then influences the results that you get. If you went in to pitch your services, or interview for a promotion, or stepped into competition to try and win a title, believing that you are an idiot who doesn't deserve success, that *will* come across and *will* affect how you navigate that opportunity and indeed may have a bearing on the outcome!

## Beware what comes after 'I am...'

When you make 'I am...' statements, you are talking about your identity. Not what you do, but who you believe you ARE. Saying 'I am...' does not make it so in reality, but your mind hears it and will always do its darnedest to make a reality out of what you feed it. If you want to tell yourself repeatedly that you're forgetful or fearful, you can bet that your mind will show you examples of where you did in fact forget something, or where you did feel fear. It doesn't matter that you rectified the situation before it had negative consequences or that when you'd been scared, you'd pushed through and conquered your fear to act anyway. No, those parts of the story would be overlooked, because they don't fit the 'I am...' narrative. Pay attention to any time you declare 'I am...' and make sure those words are ones of which you want to eat the fruit![4]

## You didn't give yourself your gifts

It's not arrogant to know what you're good at. It's the only way to be fair to yourself. Noting all your perceived weaknesses and ignoring all your strengths is not modesty. It doesn't help anyone. It's just being a jerk to yourself. And you are also modelling how-to-be-a-jerk-to-yourself for anyone watching and learning from you!

You did not decide where you would be born, when, to whom, or how. You certainly did not decide what gifts, talents and strengths to give yourself. Oh sure, you may have worked with what you've been given, but none of that stuff originated with you. None of it was your idea that you decided to bestow on yourself before you were born. Whether you believe in God or not on this point is immaterial. Either way, you didn't decide.

When you acknowledge that you have strengths, you are – at the very least – acknowledging that you're not all bad. In fact, I always tell my clients that it's downright arrogant to believe you're all bad, because you're human and we just aren't that consistent!

You have strengths and talents, you're not consistent enough to be all bad, and you did not make yourself with the gifts and talents you possess, so when you acknowledge them, you're not being a legend-in-your-own-bath-time. You're just being even-handed and seeing both sides of the coin. Here's an example. When I was in Bible college, I told a friend of mine that I wanted to get a First in my degree. (For those of you who're not familiar with the UK system, a First Class degree is the top classification you can achieve and is relatively uncommon.) His response was 'wow, that's a bit arrogant isn't it?' I asked him how was it arrogant when I didn't give myself my gifts and I was only determined to use what I had to its greatest effect? To acknowledge your gifts is gratitude, not putting others down or suggesting that you're better than them. That's not possible as we'll see in part 3.

## What you focus on you get more of

The words we use matter. They really do have power. What you say is what your mind will hear and your mind will do its darnedest to make your words your reality – and it doesn't filter out the nonsense you may think. It takes it what you feed it uncritically. Repeatedly feed it 'white flashy SUVs with panoramic sunroofs' and your mind will go 'OK, got it. You're interested in paying attention to white flashy SUVs with panoramic sunroofs' and whaddayaknow? It will soon feel like every blessed car on the road is a flashy white SUV.

Was there suddenly a huge influx of flashy white SUVs? No. You had just told your mind that you were focused on those, and your mind uncritically obliged, regardless of whether you need a new car, or whether a flashy white SUV is a suitable vehicle for you since you don't actually have a driving licence. It just shows you what you have communicated that you want to see more of.

Seeing is believing, but it is just as truthful to say that believing is seeing, since what you believe, your mind will do its darnedest to show you. Conversely, it will filter out everything that does not fit what you've asked for.

I know I've already said that in as many words in the previous section, but this is incredibly important. Fundamentally important. What you think leads to you making meaning of what you experience and having feelings connected to those meanings. Those thoughts and feelings are fuelling what you do and do not do, which is directly related to the results you experience.

**BIG** IDEA: Who you believe you are matters because it impacts what you do, how you do it, and the outcomes that you believe are possible for you. Denying your strengths is not modesty, it's false humility. You're human so you have enough flaws to be humble about without making up others!

You can know all the strategies and tactics in the world that would build you a business of world-dominating success, and yet, if deep down you have not wrestled with and settled your understanding of your own worth, you will simply not be able to force yourself to execute those strategies to their greatest effect.

Strategies and expertise matter, but as you and I both know, they are not solely what decides if someone is successful.

## If she can, you can

Roxanne Hawn is a solopreneur and freelance writer with over twenty years' experience (not to mention best-selling author) who has some great words of wisdom for you about focus and the power of your thinking to change everything:

'Women entrepreneurs receive a lot of advice, unsolicited and otherwise. Much of that advice focuses on coping mechanisms to prevent burnout as if burnout is normal, acceptable, or inevitable. Dr Kat taught me to turn my thinking around. Rather than a reactionary strategy of pacing yourself for the rigours, work, and challenges ahead, I think of it more now like a yourself-paced way of living. I choose my schedule, my workloads, what I say yes to, what I decline. I honour changes in my focus and energy each day or season without judgement or caveats. If I need to nap, I nap. If I'm on a roll with a project, I harness that momentum and maybe work late sometimes. I also prioritise the things that support being the best version of myself such as walking with my dogs, knitting, reading, or planning time simply to be.

During the early days of the pandemic, I cut my work schedule to four days each week as a coping strategy. Fast forward… and I continue to work four days. I even switched my thinking and my words away from "I only work Monday through Thursday" or "I don't work Fridays" to a more affirming message like "I'm typically available Monday through Thursday" said with the confidence that such a schedule is normal and acceptable, without anyone else's permission or blessing needed.'

None of this would have happened if Roxanne had not recognised her need for work on how she was thinking and seeing herself and her world. Once she did the work on those things, it opened up opportunities to navigate the world significantly differently. Roxanne could never have known how that work would stand her in good stead when the pandemic came along but it did, and it has. Similarly, you can't see what you will want or where you will need better thinking to help you navigate, so prepare now, do this work now. Your future self will thank you!

## 3:

# How you know what you know

YOU did not learn who you 'are' in a vacuum. In Part 2 we'll dive into those waters a little and explore who you have known yourself to be in the past, but right now we're simply going to acknowledge that the 'labels' you carry in this life were not all decided or applied by you.

## Labels

We all have lots of labels and operate in different ways at different times. For example, in no particular order, the labels I could be described with include coach, consultant, mentor, entrepreneur, wife, step-mum, daughter... and many more besides. There are also labels that I used to wear, but don't apply to me anymore, such as teenager, student, choreographer, girlfriend.

How you show up in a situation is likely to be a different version of you, depending on what you see your label to be in that context, or the role you're expected to play. Think about how different you may be when you're hanging out with old school friends versus when you're a guest speaker at a professional event. What are you more open to wearing or doing when you're on holiday far from home versus how you'd show up in your own locale?

This is not to say that you are being fake in any of those places, just that different environments bring out different aspects of you. If you've ever known someone who 'brought out the worst in you', or 'pushes all your buttons', then you know this in a negative way. Similarly, there are those people who just seem to 'get' you and understand you in a way that others don't.

A large part of how you learned who you are can be attributed to your interactions with others. That can be the words they spoke over you that encouraged or crushed you. It can be the pronouncements they made about what you were capable of or how you'd 'never' be able to achieve what you said you wanted to. You learned from their attitudes to you – where you were included and what was appreciated about you, and where you were blatantly excluded, and the apparent or perceived rationale for that.

Some of these interpretations were yours, in response to what you saw or felt from others, and even those interpretations were informed by what you already believed or by past experiences. If your head is starting to hurt at all this complexity and all these moving parts, I get it, but don't lose hope.

## The enemy of your soul

If you don't share my faith, what I'm about to say might sound a little woo, but just roll with me for a minute and see what you can usefully take from this, even if it sounds alien to your ears.

Do you believe there is good in the world? Do you believe there is evil in the world? Do you believe that good or evil are located just in a few individuals or are there some sort of forces of good and evil that reside beyond a physical-can-always-see-it-in-front-of-me sort of way?

If you look at the world and sometimes see evil in it, then I would suggest you are already seeing the fruits of evil, courtesy of the enemy of all our souls. It might not be the most pleasant thing to think about but if you look around it's easy to see that there is evil in this world. That evil, that enemy of your soul, has no interest in seeing you become the version of yourself that God knows it would light you up to become. This enemy comes like a thief to steal from you all the goodness that was supposed to be yours. Jesus puts it this way: 'A thief comes to steal and kill and destroy, but I came to give life – life in all its fullness'[5].

This might be something you have wrestled with for years, or it might be a fresh idea, but as you think about how you know who you are, I want you to think about the whispers you've battled throughout your life. Those sly words that knew exactly where your weak spots were. That voice that repeated back every word you'd long forgotten, but suddenly opened up old wounds in a fresh way causing you to pull back from taking opportunities presented to you. Some of these thoughts may be all your own but look out because some have the stench of sulphur about them! Some of those most insidious words – even if spoken by humans – belong in the pit of hell from whence they originated.[6]

Throughout the rest of this book, I am going to ask you lots of questions, each designed to explore your beliefs and inner narratives to make sure they're speaking truth to you and moving you in the direction you actually want to go. Again, I really do suggest you have a nice notebook for this so you will want to write in it. Whether you start in pencil first and then move to pen or dive straight in with a pen you like, you will get much more from this book when you work through the questions as they come up. Don't tell yourself you'll come back to them later, unless of course you're that one unicorn who actually does return to them! Most of us tell ourselves that and never do, so I want to strongly encourage you to start answering them now. If you don't have a lovely notebook to hand, start on a blank piece of paper and stick or staple it into a notebook later. No excuses, I told you this was a reader participation book, so let's go!

## OVER TO YOU

- What do you identify as 'evil' in this world?
- How do you recognise it?
- Where do you think you might have encountered the 'enemy of your soul'?
- What do you think such an enemy would want to keep you from becoming or doing?
- What do you think that enemy's best tactics would be to sabotage you from becoming or doing that thing?

### Who are you?

When all the bluster and marketing lingo is stripped away, who are you? What qualities do you possess that you're proud of? If I asked people who know you or work with you to tell me what they value about you, what would they say? If they were really gushing and making you blush with their enthusiastic praise of you, what would they be saying – even if you think they're absolutely wrong?

You know there is more in you that is yet to come out. You wouldn't be reading this if something in you was not convinced that there is something else that can be seen and shared with the world. It's perhaps even why you have wondered if there was something wrong with you that things hadn't gotten where you wanted to be already. That comparison, or perhaps the sense of time marching on, or perhaps it's that your friends all seem to be further ahead...

Quiet the noise and have a think about who YOU believe you are. You've lived with you in a way no one else has, you know all the hidden desires of your heart. You know what you've dreamt of, and even the dreams you try to squish because they sound too outrageous to even allow yourself to think about.

**BIG** IDEA: You know there is more in you that is yet to come out. Quiet the noise and have a think about who YOU believe you are. You've lived with you in a way no one else has, you know all the hidden desires of your heart.

## Whose cup of tea are you?

Whether you like it or not, you are never going to be everyone's cup of tea. You are also not able to be all things to all people: maybe your skill is high performance, or perhaps your passion is helping people who're just starting out. Neither are better than the other – we need both.

Who are you best at serving? What kind of people do you actually want to attract? Who do you really not want to work with? There are perhaps people that you need to 'release to other opportunities' because there's someone out there who they could work better with, who might be a better 'fit'. That's OK! In fact, it takes a good dose of self-awareness to see where something isn't a good fit and do something about it for the good of all concerned!

---

## OVER TO YOU

- Who do you believe you are?
- Who do you believe you're not?
- Who do you think you are best able to help, given what you've been through to date, your expertise and your passions?
- Can the 'you' you believe you are fulfil the biggest vision you have for your life and business?
- If not, what stops this current iteration of you from achieving those things?
- Put another way, who would you need to be to make more of that vision become reality?
- What changes do you need to make from who you are to who you will become?

---

# 4:

## Look where you want to go

**W**HO does your very soul whisper that you could be? You know what I mean: that daydream of possibility that may feel like it's been stubbed out. It hasn't, and you know how I know that? Because you would not be reading this book if you didn't at some level know that there is more in you that the world hasn't yet seen. You may not feel it, but your ACTIONS tell a different story. You've spent some of your hard-earned money buying this book; you've actually started to read it; and now you're well through Part 1. No matter how you feel – perhaps you feel like you may have maxed out your potential or maybe you feel like you missed your opportunity for what you really dream of – something in you still holds hope, and THAT is the piece of you that I want to invite you to fan into flame as we continue. 'Right feelings follow right actions' as a pastor I knew used to say, and he was right. Your feelings will get the memo if you keep taking the right steps, and right now, the next right step is to keep pressing in and see what God still has to show you!

## Dreams are blueprints

The dreams you have on your heart weren't put there by you. I had a 'duh' epiphany about this recently. I had taken a trip to France to prepare for an upcoming exclusive boutique retreat there, and when I came back, I was telling my coach about how long it had been a dream of mine to run these retreats... and how 'lucky' it was that I had always wanted to become fluent in French! Face, meet palm. All this time, I thought that my love of French and time spent learning it was indulgent! As if it was just my idea and a distraction I had thought up – in fact it was completely the opposite way around. When I *finally* connected the dots, I realised that my desire to learn French was part of the equipping I would need to fulfil my vision with excellence. Long before I had any inkling that running retreats in France was on the horizon, God planted a desire that would equip me when, in the future, I would be ready to run gorgeous, life-changing retreats there.

I have seen time and again with my clients that dreams are blueprints. You have to take action to bring them to reality, and of course you have to believe they are possible for you but when you tune in to the dreams God placed on your heart, it really will take you to extraordinary places.

## Wild ride

I moved to Seattle for graduate school on faith. It was probably the craziest thing I've done to date and it was an incredible, wild ride. Getting there required financial miracles, not to mention an insane experience at the visa office. I had managed to get cuts on a couple of my fingers, roughly a month before my visa interview. Visa interviews were hard to get at that time, so my appointment was set for just a few weeks before I was due to fly out to start my three-year graduate programme. These cuts on my fingertips were nasty and one in particular on my forefinger simply refused to heal. I tried everything and it would not heal. It was a mess and you could not see my fingerprint. I was freaking out because you're not supposed to go to your visa interview if you have any cuts on your fingers as they take all your fingerprints.

I was sure that going to Seattle for this programme was what God wanted for me, so, with no better option presenting itself, I went to the visa interview anyway. The man behind the counter was chirpy and asked me to put my thumb on the fingerprint reader. That was fine. Then he asked for the (injured) forefinger. 'Oh, the computer didn't like that' says he in a jolly tone. Obviously, this was no surprise to me. Instantly my palms became sweaty and my heart raced but I tried to look calm whilst inwardly fervently praying. I said to God 'If you want me to go, you need to do something right now.' There was literally nothing I could do, so I went, 'right God, it's time to go big or go home.' The chirpy man, completely oblivious to my internal palpitations and rapid prayer said 'let's try that again... OK... next finger... ' My legs nearly went from under me. I KNOW it shouldn't have been a shock since I had prayed for this exact thing and knew it was possible, but there's a difference between intellectually knowing God can do something and having it happen right there in the moment! I got the visa and I went to Seattle as scheduled. I could fill a book with the crazy things that happened during those three years as God got me through it. It was a week by week, month by month leap of faith, and I cannot encourage you enough to experience one – or a life – of these leaps of faith for yourself. I'll tell you one more of the crazy stories later in the book, but what I want you to get from this is that, unlike the baptised-in-pickle-juice tame impression you may have been given by some about God, in my experience, nothing is further from the truth. If God has put something on your heart, trust Him for it. If He confirms again and again that you're made for a particular path – even if you don't see how it could be possible – trust Him. Making things possible is far above your pay grade to worry about. Knock it upstairs and do what is humanly within your control, and seriously, lean on God for the rest. Just like He did in that simple example of my mashed-up finger with its indistinguishable fingerprint, He is an absolute hoot! If it's His plan for you, He will make a way even where everything within you screams 'there is no way!' As CS Lewis put it, 'He's not safe, but He is good.'[7]

Time to get your notebook out again because I have questions.

---

## OVER TO YOU

- What dreams are on your heart – however crazy or impractical they may seem? If you weren't limited to worldly means, what could be possible for you?
- Ask God to remind you of dreams He's previously put on your heart that He wants to rekindle. Sit with that for a minute. What comes to mind?

---

### Look where you want to go

When I lived in Washington State, USA, I wanted to learn to snowboard. Luckily for me, I was able to get special offers and catch a bus from close by my house to take me up to the local ski area, because there's no way my wee beaten-up car would have made it, even if I could've found the money for snow chains!

Off I trotted at every opportunity I could to take lessons and practice. I'd like to say I ended up being really good but I *really* didn't. On one notable occasion, even in my helmet, I managed to crack my head on the beginner's practise slope, and of course I did that on a day when it was like an ice rink. Cue a two-week headache (read: probably concussion). The fact that I couldn't afford to visit a doctor will be no surprise to US readers, but for those used to the NHS like I am, it sure makes you realise what a gem that is, and how downright dangerous wealth-based/insurance-limited healthcare can be. I digress.

In one notable lesson, I was on the bunny run which has what feels like a short steep slope (if you're a wuss, and I definitely am) that leads down on to a really flat bit of the run, before going down a final hill that takes you back to the bottom. Off to the right of this flat bit is what, in my memory, I have immortalised as a 'drop off'. It's an area with trees, and, at the time, orange plastic fencing that sat between the unwary (or woefully poor) snowboarder/skier and those trees. Bear in mind that my recollection of this 'drop off' owes more to my active imagination, ineptitude and general fear than it does to reality! This was a beginner run, undoubtedly safe as it was used by thousands each year. But my imagination interpreted it very differently! Let the reader understand that reality be damned, what matters here is how my brain was interpreting the scene.

I'm a geek, so I had done my homework prior to first attending a lesson and I had learned that landing up in snowy trees was really not a good place to be. Very dangerous, in fact – it was suggested as somewhere you definitely want to avoid. Bear that in mind for what follows.

I also should tell you that I (attempt to) ride a board 'goofy', which means that I ride with my right leg forward and, when I'm using my heel edge of the board, the board is going to curve me off to the right, whilst 'regular' riders will more naturally curve off to the left.

Again, this is a relevant detail.

So there I was at the top of this 'steep' wee slope, ready to rock. I was enjoying the lesson, the instructor was brilliant and I was feeling more confident. So I attacked the slope and felt like I was flying as I came down it! I hurtled towards the flat bit. I say 'hurtled' but I'm reasonably confident that 'hurtled' could more accurately be described as 'like a turtle stampeding through molasses'. Still, it felt fast to this turtle.

For once, I reckoned I'd be able to get the whole way across the flat bit without coming to a mortifying stop and having to shuffle along it or take my board off and walk. For a moment it felt amazing. Then I noticed that everyone else was curving off to the left, away from the orange fencing and the trees. Come to think of it, I was heading TOWARDS the drop off! NOOOOO...

So, in my usual understated manner, I guldered across to my instructor 'I'M HEADING TOWARDS THE EDGE!!'

Her advice which was going to – in my head – save my life?

'Don't look at it!!!'

My inner dialogue had some choice words, but audibly I managed a 'WHAT?!'

'Do you want to go over the edge and into the trees?' she asked me. If I'd not been hurtling towards a veritable chasm with a board strapped to my feet, I'd possibly have had a more eloquent response, but as it was I yelled, 'NO!!!' *You maniac, of COURSE I don't want to end up like a human popsicle wrapped in orange fencing and head first into the deep snow by a tree where certain death awaits! What kind of advice is this?!!!* These are all the things I did NOT say, though I am confident that my face displayed them.

Calmly still, she asks, 'Well, where do you want to go?' I gestured wildly over to the left where all the rest of the lemmings/learners were going. 'OK, so look over there and that's where you'll go,' says she. For some reason, instead of resorting to my usual methods of braking (butt-plant and face-plant), I trusted her. Lo and behold, I curved off to the left and lived to tell the tale. She was right: where I looked was where I went. What made the difference was to look where I wanted to go, instead of expending all that wasted energy focusing on where I didn't want to go.

I've told this story in multiple countries and what is fun is how many people have had stories from different sports that tell the same story: where you focus is where you go. One client told me how he used to compete on a motorbike, and how he had always been told that you should never look at the wall unless you want to go into it. Similarly, equestrian clients of mine have said that they train their eye line for jumping to clear the jumps, rather than end up on the ground by looking at the base of the jump. A ski competitor client said how she'd always been told to ignore the trees...

Whether it's sport that you're thinking of, or your perspective on yourself or your purpose, where you focus matters because where you focus is where you'll go.

Have you ever gone out in your car and ended up taking the wrong direction because you were thinking about somewhere else? It's easily done. When you're not intentionally concentrating on where you want to go, you can easily end up going a different direction by default. That's where it is wise to have someone skilled to come alongside you, someone who can help you identify what's taking you the wrong direction and can guide you to re-focus where you *actually* want to go, with specific strategies to help you get there.

---

## OVER TO YOU

- Are you focused on where you want to go, or have you been focused on what you're worried about?
- What direction *do* you want to go?
- What do you need to change so that you're moving in the direction you want to go?
- How can you fix your eyes on that outcome?
- Who helps you course correct when you're heading in the wrong direction or get stuck on a flat plateau?

---

## What lights you up?

What excites you now may not be the same as it was when you were a child. Your personal and professional interests may have moved on significantly too. I've seen this for myself in my life so far. None of the learning or the experiences are wasted – it all informs what I bring to this work I do now and absolutely love.

You've been thinking about who you are, so before we turn our attention to what and who has helped you become who you are, I want you to take a moment and write a brain dump of everything that you have in this moment, everything that you are, everything that you love. Take time to assess everything that is going well and that you're grateful for – no matter how silly you think others might consider it or how seemingly small it is. When you do this, think about all aspects of your life, from personal to professional, experiential to existential.

What is working well? What intrigues you? What excites you? What are you so enthusiastic about that you can't stop talking about? What are you curious to learn more about? Who and what makes you smile?

Gratitude is an overlooked superpower, but while you're looking at who you are and how you're showing up in the world, it can be easy to see where you have room to grow and feel lacking. But there is so much potential in you, so much as yet unwritten and I want you to feel like you're an incredible gift that someone should be absolutely busting to get to unwrap or work with.

Once you've done this exercise with gusto, it's time to take that fabulous you and explore how you got to this point. Then, in Part 3, we'll tie it all together and step into future you. OK, brain dump first, then ONWARD!

# PART 2: Who were you?

# 5:

# Who you are is not who you were

HOW did you get to be who you are today, as the person who thinks how you think? Who helped shape your thinking? Who imparted knowledge that stuck with you?

One of my bugbears with some of the coaching world is how individualistic it is. I mean, a solely individualistic focus might be fine if you lived on a desert island and had never come into contact with another living soul (obviously in this scenario, you'd not have come into contact with me or this book, but hey, what's a little impossibility to get in the way of the 'self-made' narrative?) Since that's absolute nonsense, we need to acknowledge the simple fact that you HAVE come into contact with the world – both sentient and otherwise – which has led you to conclusions about life, the world and your place in it. Those deep-seated values[8], beliefs, principles, *worldview* are the map you use to guide your attitudes and actions in everything you do, and have done, to this point. If we ignore all the influences on you and pretend that you just conjured up your worldview in a God-like out of nothing kind of way, then it stands to reason that you are culpable for all the errors along the way. Whilst I am never going to remove your responsibility to do the best you can with what you know and then to do better when you know better, some of the beliefs you hold have come from outside of you and this is important because it's easier to solve a problem when you don't feel like you are a problem. By examining some of the influences that have shaped you, you'll be able to apply that to stories from your past and show yourself more grace for your part in them, or understand better how others helped you reach the heights that you did. The past is not finished. The attitudes and learning you gleaned – whether helpful or unhelpful – continue to inform your actions, unless and until you intentionally decide to change them. By understanding the 'subplots' of some of your past stories and throwing light on the 'supporting roles' played by others, you will gain a richer perspective on who you have already been, which you can then recruit for the present and into the future.

## Identifying all the characters

We all have principles that guide how we look at the world, what we expect from it, and how we make decisions. Whilst your particular cocktail may have nuances that differ from others around you, it is easy to see that the values you hold are not unique to you. The principles, moral standards and the expectations you have for yourself and others are honed and developed within a broader context. Your values have also likely changed and developed as you grew into adulthood and over the course of your life so far, whether having gained new insight or information from your interactions with others that changes your beliefs, or in reaction to something you saw that you felt passionately opposed to. The influences on your thinking and those who've educated you could be close family, extended family, subcultures of school, work or church, society, or these days, perhaps it's TV and Internet that have helped formed your view of the world. Some of what you know is informed by what you saw modelled for you by others – for example, aspirational women who have blazed a trail and showed you what it looked like to achieve particular heights and positions. Before I went to theatre school, I grew up hearing about others who'd gone from our back water part of the world before and had successful careers. Occasionally one of them would return and take class during our Summer School locally, and when they would dance, we'd crowd around the windows to watch them. They showed what was possible if you worked hard enough and dared to dream big enough.

You perhaps also had your values formed in reaction to something you experienced, so that you decided to take actions that are polar opposites to what you grew up with. This often shows up in parenting decisions and trying to provide your children with what you didn't have. When I was training as a therapist, I heard heroic stories of parents who were struggling, yet who were managing to give their children what they'd never experienced for themselves. I always found that ability to conjure up a different way forward, when it was so alien to them personally, to be awe-inspiring.

### 'All animals are equal...'

You'll probably recognise the famous extract of a quote here as being from George Orwell's *Animal Farm*. The pigs start out after their rebellion saying 'All animals are equal' but over time, their greed and tyranny develop and change the ethos to 'All animals are equal, but some are more equal than others'.

Whilst we're discussing the influences on you, let's just take a beat to acknowledge explicitly that those influences are not neutral. Orwell's allegory was about political power, but let's not kid ourselves that selfish motives, greed or downright malevolence are the sole preserve of politicians. For example, it is generally accepted that murder is not OK. Generally, it is accepted as being a bad thing.

However, although 'All animals are equal' may be the sentiment in society and law, in reality, the subtext can be more akin to Orwell's pigs' latter pronouncement, that some are more equal than others. There are underlying assumptions, prejudices and weightings given to different murderers and victims, such as the woeful continuing rush to excuse and explain away 'domestic' murders or sexual assaults where the perpetrator is a 'respectable' white male or a celebrity. The same consideration and preference would not be given to men of lesser stature or with darker skin, or to women. This bias is also seen where women are perceived as having 'triggered' or caused their own victimisation, in the nauseating 'she had just ended their marriage...' or 'she was out late', 'she had been drinking', 'she was wearing a thong'. I can assure you these are not exaggerations. All of these statements have been used to blame women for the acts of violence perpetrated against them, which speaks to some values of society, albeit less savoury ones.

These prejudices have ramifications. Even where, for example, racism or misogyny are not written law, these attitudes of heart will leak out. This is why beliefs are so important. At some level we know the values of the culture we live in and often unconsciously make choices to aid survival or avoid censure and attack, whether physical or metaphorical.

Gavin De Becker explains in his book *The Gift of Fear: Survival Signals that protect us from violence*, 'It is understandable that the perspectives of men and women on safety are so different – men and women live in different worlds. I don't remember where I first heard this simple description of one dramatic contrast between the genders, but it is strikingly accurate: At core, men are afraid women will laugh at them, while at core, women are afraid men will kill them.'[9]

This may seem a heavy place to go with this idea, but if we don't acknowledge the big and weighty places where you instinctively may have learned to hold back, how can you honour what you have achieved despite that context, and give yourself grace to grow in tender understanding of why you've felt compelled to make the choices you have? Because those choices did not occur in a vacuum.

## You don't exist in a vacuum

You do not exist in a vacuum. As I said before, you did not get to this point in life without interactions with the world around you. What I love is that at no point can you credibly see yourself as an *individual* without reference to all the people who have got you this far. I love that we are interconnected and this inter-dependence is one of the wonders and frustrations of life.

You are, in part, the product of generations of genes, of a family context, of educational establishments, of friendship groups, and more. And beyond all those known and named connections, you also exist in a particular time in history.

The world you were born into has a history and, depending on your sex, you arrived into a world that had pre-existing notions of what a person of that sex would be like, what they would do, a whole set of societal norms, in fact, that this baby would learn, be shaped by and come to understand the costs of transgressing those norms.

You were born into a particular time in history, but not without that history. From the circumstances of your conception, through your development during pregnancy, birth story and beyond, nothing that happened to bring you into this world occurred without involving a story and the history of those whose actions resulted in you being here. Once you were born, you were born into a world that from the get-go had a mental picture of how they should treat you, depending on your sex. For example, research has shown that adults introduced to a crying baby interpreted the cry differently, depending whether they believed the child to be male or female.[10]

Your caregivers – whether parent(s), foster parent(s) or other guardian(s) – all had their own history and upbringing, their own expectations of children and values around the place of each in the family dynamic and the broader world. The social context you were in also has norms and expectations of people in that circle. This context also held stories, such as about the importance (or not) of education and what to expect from life. Did they believe that high achievement was possible or was success not for 'people like them' or 'people who come from here'? Perhaps their perspective was focused on sex and what the expectations were for you as a girl, and later, as a woman?

You learned the norms, practices, traditions, expectations and rules of this social context and much of it was never openly spoken about. There is much that you learn along the way through what is unspoken, or obliquely navigated by others, whose behaviours you then grow up 'catching'.

What this means is that the 'you' reading this book has been shaped by many forces, some of which we haven't even mentioned yet – and between the interactions of all those influences, your experiences, your own personality and character have interplayed until here you are. You have never existed in a vacuum and what helps or hinders you now is also a product of everything leading to this point.

### If she can, you can

Integrated movement specialist and Pilates studio owner Stacy Weeks says: 'My business and my personal life have been blessed through my interactions with Dr Kat. I signed up for her Mastermind programme in 2021 to get more in depth with my business. What I got was more than I ever imagined. The wins for my business were utterly fantastic, but out of all the awards, articles and professional recognition my business received, the personal journey was the most profound win. There were tears, sometimes tantrums but I felt confident discussing all manner of uncomfortable moments as a group and in my 1:1 coaching sessions. The personal growth armed me to deal with two of the worst years of my life that saw pandemic enforced business closures, financial struggles, dog sickness and divorce. My businesses both in person and online are here today in many ways due to the support I had from working with Dr Kat. I feel more confident which has given me the courage to put myself out there professionally, develop business ideas and use my voice. The personal enlightenment was a real bonus, I never saw that coming, and it is one I'm truly grateful for receiving.'

What Stacy discovered was the interaction between business and the rest of life. It might sound obvious, but too often business development is taught as if it can be kept separate from the rest of life, as if the rest sits neatly boxed up until you've finished with making money. That's a nonsense of course. You're one whole person and you live a whole life that needs to be taken into account if you're not going to burn out. It needs to be intentionally crafted if you want to go further and actually live a rich, sustainable, thriving life.

This is why I am so passionate about intentionality and awareness – both of the self, and of the interaction between your own self and the self of others. These factors matter. It drives me crazy when coaches act as if you exist as an individual who only has to think positive enough thoughts and have a high enough vibe to 'spiritually bypass' the mundanity of life and connectedness. It's nonsense and it does you a massive disservice, not to mention you live in a world that really needs you not be navel gazing in self-focused oblivion.

When you wrap your brain around who you were, who you are and who you were created to be, it will not only transform your coaching and leadership, it will be transformative for your clients and others you interact with. You will never look at yourself or them the same way again.

## OVER TO YOU

- Who and what has influenced you most up to this point? As you have read this chapter, what stories from your past came to mind?
- What do you believe about this world and your place in it? Where do you see limitations for 'someone like you'?
- Do you accept those limitations or do you want to find a way to defy them?
- Where do you see possibilities for 'someone like you'?
- What do you wish you'd been taught about what 'someone like you' is capable of? As you think about who you've been in the past and the contexts you found yourself in, what themes do you see emerging?
  **Hint:** look for themes that someone who really supports and believes in you would see. This is not about re-hashing negative old stories that don't serve you. If you can't think of someone who'd point out the strengths that exist in past stories, imagine I am there with you. Trust me when I tell you that I am stubborn and I would not rest until I found the nuggets of gold I know live in some of your past stories, so mentally recruit me to the task as you need to!

*'I became a rebel. I used to wear my school skirt so high you would have thought it was a serviette. I was marvellous. I used to exude boredom from every pore and I hated everything.'*[11]

*Shirley Valentine* is a play by Willy Russell that was turned into a fantastic movie with gorgeous scenery and tells the story of the eponymous Shirley Valentine, a woman who used to be rebellious and brave and fierce, and who has somehow lost sight of herself in the intervening years and what happens when she gets the opportunity to see her life from a different perspective. I work with a lot of women who can identify with elements of this quote. Somewhere along the lines, they lost their fierceness or their audacity to go against others' expectations. Sometimes the sense of loss is for the naïvety of youth when you believed anything was possible, and now you feel compelled to do what is expected and pretend it's what you want to do. Whether you identify with Shirley here or not, most of us can recognise that the person we are now is not the same person we were at earlier stages of life. Sometimes that's a sad realisation, but at other times you look at who you were then and realise that those changes are a really good thing! These changes from then to now are what I want you to consider now.

## You weren't always who you are now

Sometimes we grow in some areas of life yet in other areas we seem to shrink back. Perhaps when you were younger, you were really fearless and would take on any climbing feat or adventure that came your way... but now you're a lot more cautious.

Maybe it's the other way round. Perhaps you used to be shy and wouldn't have spoken in front of a crowd and now you love speaking gigs and the bigger audience, the better! We all change as we go along, sometimes in ways that help us, and other times, perhaps the pendulum swings a little too far, and we could do with getting back a little of a characteristic we once had in spades. How you see yourself is dynamic and changes as you grow up. When I was little, I wanted to be Wonder Woman or Princess Leia. I would've been happy with either. I didn't see myself as strong or brave or fierce like them, but I loved those qualities in them. Whilst I'm not often (ever) to be seen running around in wrist cuffs, a bustier and a tiara like Wonder Woman, I recognise that others have seen some of those characters' characteristics in me, and my sense of self now acknowledges that there are things I have done already in life that some might consider strong or brave or fierce. That's the thing about our evolving sense of self though: it is sometimes informed by others' perception of us – at least in part – and yet sometimes we write off what others see because it doesn't fit with how we see ourselves. Or we take it for granted and don't think it qualifies as 'brave' or 'strong' because it was just something we did or something we survived. Too often familiarity with ourselves breeds contempt. If you're engaging in personal development through studying, coaching, mentorship, therapy or just plain old living-and-learning, your sense of self will likely change and develop along the way. On a life trajectory, the stories you believe about yourself will change because your sense of self has changed and grown, and with maturity/experience, you'll interpret events differently too. You also may find that in different contexts or with different people, different traits came to the fore. For example, that person who 'brings out the worst in you' or that teacher who inspires you.

## Who did you used to be?

Let me give you an example. When I was in secondary school, I had to take technology class which involved engineer-type design and using all sorts of machines that required safety briefings[12]. I HATED technology and I was not good at it. One year my report read, 'Kathrine *has* done some good work this year' and the emphasis made me laugh, because my teacher really had to search for something good to say about my woeful attempts at designing structures or using a lathe or soldering iron. However, Mr Ievers was also the director of the school plays, and they were fantastic. I was a cheeky brat who loved to verbally spar with him and enjoyed the banter. I was always to his face about it, never spoke behind his back, and I had the utmost respect for him as the acting dude. Performing was what I lived and breathed for, so he was the gatekeeper to a wonderful world where I could be someone else and actually feel at peace in my own skin, albeit under the guise of a character.

When not on a stage, that teenage Kathrine absolutely hated herself, but when she was bantering with this teacher who seemed to understand and enjoy her attitude (rather than finding it frustrating or irritating as some of the other teachers clearly – and understandably! – did), getting roles in the plays that were a JOY, and feeling like she actually was doing something well... that self-loathing awkward teenager was someone else. I don't look back on that girl and feel the self-loathing. I see, I feel, the girl who was quick with a sassy retort and who could act well. She felt nerves as she stood at the side of the stage, and often felt like her mind was blank, uncertain of her first line when she stepped out on stage, but every time, she stepped out there and right into the flow of the part. It felt amazing. Exhilarating. And that memory of standing in the wings (back far enough that even my feet couldn't be seen, because he drilled that into us as part of his 'cues, diction, discipline, projection' credo)... that memory of standing there completely consciously clueless as to what came next has powered me through so many speaking engagements since, because I KNOW that I have got this and can trust the process.

Seeing yourself as you were with people who believed in you can be tremendously powerful even years later, even if your sense of self has been challenged in between times. It's not always the most obvious people either who show you a side to yourself that you can recruit to take forward. Don't forget, you're still inhabiting the same body as you were at earlier points in your life. You are older, but you're still you. You may have changed, but you've already been those versions of you that you remember, so when there are skills and traits that you feel you need for the road ahead, you may find that it's not that you need to learn alien traits for the first time, but rather that you may be able to dust off long-neglected ones, or read again once familiar stories of who you were, are and can be.

## OVER TO YOU

- At different stages of your life, who were you with different people who knew you well and cared about you?
- Think about your home life, and who you were in your local community. Who were you when you were with your friends or at school, doing hobbies or at different jobs you've had along the way?
- Who spoke encouraging words over you or inspired you from afar?
- Who have you proved wrong in their assessment or expectations of you?
- What aspects of you have come to light as you've thought back over your life so far? Which of these traits might you want to recruit as we go forward?

## Forgive past you

Who you are as you show up in the world right now is informed by what you've learned and who you've been in the past. As you look back on who you've been or even consider who you are today, don't be surprised if a whisper comes up trying to evoke shame for who you were or where you perhaps lost the run of yourself at times and haven't shown up in all your brilliance.

As you grow, it is normal to need to exercise a little forgiveness, not least of yourself. In all probability you did the best you knew how to do with the resources, wisdom, maturity and skills that you possessed at the time. The fact that you wish you could go back and do things differently is proof of your growth, is it not?! Just as you may need to forgive others for their actions, you may need to show yourself compassion. As someone who used to be absolutely vicious to herself, I know that this can seem impossible, but trust me when I tell you that it IS possible. At the very least, it is something worthy of getting coaching around, if not therapy. And if you're ready to bring the big guns in, I definitely recommend you letting God loose on you. His determination to teach me that I'm not worthless and that He even enjoys me has been quite the campaign, and one I am glad I let Him loose on! If that's not your jam, do the work so you can live free of shame and regret. As for forgiving others, I recognise that it may feel so raw that forgiveness for heinous acts feels like letting someone off the hook. It's not about them though, and it doesn't mean you can't see justice. The point of forgiveness is not merely for that other person, it's so that you are freed from the snares of hatred, bitterness and continuing to have your life defined by their actions. Forgiveness is important even for perceived 'minor' misdeeds. I tell my clients often to give others grace when they mess up, because you'll mess up sometime soon and you'll need grace from others! Us humans are spectacularly talented at making a hash of things, both intentionally and unintentionally, and a little grace to think the best of people and allow for their humanness can go a long way. That allowance for 'human' moments applies to you too.

## 6:

## The socialisation of men and women

*'What are little boys made of?*
*What are little boys made of?*
*Snips and snails*
*And puppy-dogs' tails*
*That's what little boys are made of*

*What are little girls made of?*
*What are little girls made of?*
*Sugar and spice*
*And all things nice*
*That's what little girls are made of'*

THIS old rhyme sums up a truth that research has backed up time after time: from the outset, males and females are treated differently and have differing expectations placed on them. Whether those expectations are set by those closest to them, friends, school, church or society more generally, each sex is born into this context.

Girls are still groomed with clothes following a 'sugar and spice and all things nice' gender 'norm' or expectation. If you doubt me, just look at the T-shirts in an average store, and the messages on them aimed at girls. If you made a drinking game of taking a shot every time you found an exhortation to a girl to 'be kind', you'd do yourself an injury in no time! Compare those messages to the ones on T-shirts designed for boys and I challenge you to find a single 'be kind' in the midst of all the action packed, can do, rough-and-tumble messages aimed at boys. Girls are trained and expected to mould themselves around others and keep them happy. At the same time, the common phrase 'boys will be boys' glosses over all manner of offences committed by the male of the species. If this sex-delineated, limitation-filled grooming of girls didn't irritate the snot out of you before now, I hope it will when you see it in future. It's a walloping big part of what taught you that you weren't enough, that taught you what you 'couldn't' do, and what suggested you should dream smaller. Gender norms never cared who you really were, let alone who you were created to be, but they're one more barrier put in everyone's way, and I do mean everyone.

Let me put this even more clearly: this hurts men too. This limiting stereotyping is harmful for *both* sexes. Think of how limited the permissible scope of emotions for a man is. A 'real' man is permitted which emotions without losing face? Hmm, lust, anger, love on his wedding day maybe, grief at a funeral? He's supposed to 'man up', not be a [insert derogatory term for female anatomy] by talking about his feelings or struggling. THAT is harmful, and a weight that no man should have to bear. That's why I say that the limitations imposed by 'gender' are ultimately harmful for everyone. But for now, let's return our focus to women and how females are socialised.

There are traits seen as 'to be expected' in a man. The same traits in a woman may be a source of ridicule, scorn or censure. For example, the old chestnut that a man in work strongly expressing their opinion is showing 'leadership' or is 'assertive', whereas a woman may be criticised for being 'aggressive', a negative connotation though the action and degree of forcefulness are the same. Women have a reputation for being talkers, yet in business meetings, women have been shown to speak less, and for shorter periods[13]. They also do more tasks beyond their job description than men[14], otherwise they are seen as not being a 'team player'[15].

The research is clear: women do more housework than men, on top of their jobs for which they still do not receive equal pay. Women doing the same job as male peers can still expect to be paid approximately 0.81 cents to the US dollar for the same work[16]. Women are also still discriminated against in interviews for positions and promotions (yes, even where that is technically illegal) for being child-bearing age, as the assumption is that they will want to have children[17], and when a child is ill, it will be the female who is expected to drop everything to care for them. Bear in mind that none of this is necessarily *at all* what suits or serves individual families, and there are plenty of fathers who wish it were accepted for them to look after their children as needed. Notice how you may already be seeing how unacceptable this would seem in some contexts, and the questions it may raise as to why the mother wasn't stepping up to look after them.

Even when raised in a more egalitarian home, with no intentional bias, women are still raised within a wider culture with a strong and often unspoken understanding of the roles and expectations of that society for each sex – and transgressing those norms comes at a cost. Their parent(s) or guardian(s) also learned the norms in their society as they were growing up, so none of this learning is happening without a broader context with generational ripples and adjustments over time. These 'norms' of roles and expectations play out in schools, friendship groups, churches, clubs and throughout all interactions in society. The norms get learned and learned well.

As the global Covid-19 pandemic hit in 2020, it was women who were disproportionately being impacted, often being in lower paid jobs to begin with, and more likely to be more greatly affected by lockdowns[18]. They are expected to be the primary caregivers and so if they had children, they were likely now having to take on home-schooling duties and more childcare on top of previous responsibilities, even if they are working from home. My clients quickly had to find new routines and spaces to accommodate their work and the sudden school environment too. Though many of their husbands/partners would have been happy to step up, the opportunities were not necessarily open to them, and this lack of opportunity for fathers can also be detrimental and frustrating to them too. The sexist assumptions around gender roles hurt both sexes and end up limiting opportunities for *both*. I hope you are picking up in all of this that none of this is to be down on men. Men get hurt in this paradigm too. That said, I'm not finished highlighting what you probably already have experienced navigating, to a greater or lesser extent (or have witnessed others having to navigate), as a woman in this world.

Women are also the most affected when their work does require them to be physically present, if childcare is not available. The financial and emotional pressures of these stereotyped norms hurts both sexes and puts different pressures on both individually, not to mention relationally.

Add to this the expectation that women will be the emotional caretaker in the home. It is women who are often expected to make the peace, to calm things down, to protect the male ego and not challenge the status quo. I know we'd all like to believe that this is a caricature of the emotional responsibility placed on women, but the continuing low conviction rate for sexual offences by men against women, the level of violence against women and the widespread exoneration of men whilst victim-blaming women, all very much show that the 'she provoked me' line of shifting responsibility for male emotions to women is alive and well, unlike many of its victims.

It's no wonder then that after managing her home, partner and children, a woman finds her tank empty when she comes to start the business that is on her heart, or she finds herself weary before she even begins to grow it to what it could potentially be.

When I say 'managing' her partner, I mean emotional care taking, as well as the mental load of all the seemingly small things that need to be done and are left undone until she either does them herself or puts them on her partner's to do list (and risk the accusation of 'nagging'). Again: I do not say this to be down on men. These very same dynamics ultimately stunt men's growth and, I would argue, create relational conflict which stymies intimacy. The status quo actually hurts men and women, even where it promotes or at least gives the appearance of serving men. Your personal experience may align with much or little of this, but in general, these are ways that the water still flows, so even if you are not directly swimming in their flow, you are contextually still experiencing their wake. None of this is to say that you are powerless or should just sit down under the weight of gender expectations. Quite the opposite. But I want you to recognise the dross that you have to wade through and give yourself some credit for all the barriers you may be pushing out of your way in order to be who the good Lord put YOU here to be. Recognise the norms, even if you reject them, or if you decide to accept them, then at least do so in recognition of what you've signed up to!

In the societal context I've just briefly described, is it really surprising that women learn to doubt themselves? When they spend their days being 'nice' and making sure everyone else has their physical and emotional needs met, are we really going to feign surprise when she feels guilt?

**BIG** IDEA: Context matters. You don't become who you are by yourself. As you grow into the juiciest version of who you can become, don't be surprised if not everyone gets it. The fun bit is that others will. Put yourself in environments with those who will cheer on your growth and worth.

Guilt about prioritising, no, not even prioritising, *acknowledging* her own needs and engaging in her own self-care?

OF COURSE she doubts herself.

OF COURSE she fears upsetting people.

OF COURSE it's intimidating to unleash her intellect.

OF COURSE the idea of unbridling her passion is fearsome.

How could it be anything else? She has been such a successful student of societal norms. This is how she's been trained. It's how she's survived this far and had the degree of acceptance that she has. To unfurl her passion, unfold her fury and to give vent to her fully embodied womanhood in all its glory is going to scare the pants off people. And she knows it. You know it too. It's why speaking up feels like a high-stakes decision. Yet to stay small and silent is not to be fully you as God intended and forces you to squeeze yourself into a smaller life that He never intended for you.

## A word on women and church

Depending on your religious tradition (if you have one), you may have wondered how this stuff fits within a Biblical paradigm. That's a big question, and one I am not even going to try to answer fully here, because it is complex, and many people come to many different conclusions.

For me, my bottom line is that if you feel God calling you to something and human rules try to prevent you from doing that, you have a choice to make: Please humans or please God. I know which one I want to please, though I'd really rather if I could do both at the same time! Ah, simplistic heart, if only. I am not here to privilege business over homemaking, or home-schooling and parenting over a non-parent who is out there being their fabulous self in the world. The world needs us all. I believe God created us all uniquely, and that includes to our unique purpose.

To put it in Biblical terms, I believe we're all created to be functioning members of the one body, we're *supposed* to be different and fulfilling different roles. We've just got this nasty habit of wanting people to be like us and think like us.

What you've learned about who it is 'acceptable' to be may owe more to power dynamics and what suits others than it does to who God made you to be. There may be some un-learning to do along the way. As you continue to dive into your stories and remember who you've been, keep looking out for places to interrogate the assumptions fuelling your actions. This will help you as we look at who you are being in the world right now. Other than that, who am I to tell you what God has in store for you?

As we wrap up Part 2, I want to walk you through some questions that I use when I am mentoring, to give you an opportunity to look at a specific important event from your past that relates to something you believe about yourself. Keep this as light as you want, or go as deep as you feel comfortable, and think of one specific event and how you viewed it then, the perspectives that might also be valid, and how you can recruit knowledge gleaned to help you in future.

Now look, I get that there are big questions here and you may want to gloss over them, but in the answers you will find connections you've never made before, AHAs and moments of such rich epiphany that they have the power to give you major breakthroughs. So when you feel the resistance and want to skip on, grab your notebook and get writing. Don't miss this opportunity for AHAs whether this is your first, second or fifth time through this book

## OVER TO YOU

- What happened? *For example, my teacher said I'd never cut it in business as I wasn't tough enough.*
- What did you learn about yourself? *I'm too weak to succeed at making money.*
- Who helped you come to that conclusion? *My teacher. Also my friend who said that I am too quiet to be able to speak to customers.*
- Why might they have believed that in their flawed humanness? *They don't run a business. They were imagining the qualities they expect a business owner to have. They didn't know me well enough to know how determined I am.*
- Who would not have agreed with that interpretation? *Anyone who I had ever convinced to buy cookies from me, when they really didn't need them. My parents.*
- What evidence might they have presented to back up their perspective which contradicts your understanding at the time? *The cookie buyers could point to their receipts or their waist line (I was really persuasive). My parents would point to my bedtime negotiation skills.*
- What other interpretations could there have been? *The teacher couldn't imagine a woman running a successful business. The teacher was trying to protect me from failure or disappointment. The teacher knew business can be tough and didn't want to give any of us false hope...*
- What do you wish others had known at that time? *That being soft is not all there is to know about me.*
- Looking back as an adult now, how can you understand things differently? *I can recognise that they only saw me once a week and what they saw didn't look like a stereotypical business owner.*

- What difference does that make to your thinking or how it feels in your body? *It feels lighter, like a weight lifted off me.*
- Is the belief you learned in that past experience still relevant today?
- If not, what is true instead?
- If yes, where is the recent evidence?
- Does holding on to this old belief help you to become who you want to be?
- If not, what evidence from more recent history can you think of that defies this picture of you?

---

There's a lot in all those questions. When I work with my clients, obviously I don't hit them with all those questions straight after each other, but within the limits of a book, I want to make sure you at least have the beginning of an understanding of how you can do this for yourself, because being able to look back and re-examine what you learned in the past can help you disempower some of the unhelpful beliefs and thinking that has been holding you back.

Now that we've looked at you now and in the past, it's time to look ahead, to who you are becoming.

# PART 3: Who were you created to be?

# 7:

## Look up

IN the first two parts of this book, you've looked at who you are being at this point in your life, and who you've been at different points in the past. The whole way along, we've been looking at ways you can gain a richer understanding of who you are and what you have learned so that you'll begin to see just how much you matter, and how purposed you are to be *you*, not merely a carbon copy of someone else.

Now it's time to look ahead and for this, we're unashamedly going to look not within – as you're often told to do – but look UP. If you're not sure about the whole God thing, firstly, thank you for reading this far. Secondly, keep going. Yes, I am going to drop more Jesus in this section, so take what you want from it and leave the rest. Your beliefs are your homework to do and this whole book is about working out who *you* are, including when you encounter someone like me who may think wildly differently on some things. I have so much respect for you for doing this work and I know that God loves the stink out of us both.

## You're not on your own

*'I lift up my eyes to the hills – from where will my help come?*
*My help comes from the Lord, who made heaven and earth.'*[19]

I love this verse. My logo is in part designed to reflect it. The mountains are what I look to and when I do, I always think of this verse. It's a reminder to me that I don't do any of this in my own strength, but that I am reliant on God who actually has strength and who made everything, including me. So much of what we are generally coached to believe is that we have everything within us, that you have it all just buried within you waiting to come out, if only you just have the right coaching or strategy to unlock it. But what if, instead of looking within, you were freed from having to save yourself? What if actually you were never intended to have all the answers, and you could release yourself from the pressure of having to look within all the time. Maybe it's just me, but there was a time when looking within felt like looking into the void and expecting answers from my own depleted resources was an exhausting idea. Call me lazy, but I really like not having to be the source of all wisdom I rely upon. These days I take real comfort in knowing that much of what I want to do is above my pay grade to worry about. If God puts a dream on my heart, then I am going to need God to make it happen, because the wildest of my dreams are beyond what is humanly possible for me. It's not my job to do everything, but to start moving in that direction and expect that if God wants it to come to fruition, He is going to show up and do something beyond my capacity to make it happen. I recognise that this is tricky if you're diametrically opposed to the idea of God, but if I can cast a vision for you of life beyond a sort of 'you're on your own' type model, I'd like to cast it for you.

As I've said throughout this book, if you're not sure what you think about God, or if you've decided to follow a different worldview than mine, I invite you to keep reading and take what you can from these pages, even if the faith bit is not your cup of tea. This section may feel like it's a continuation of the 'present you' but there is a shift that I want you to catch. We're going to look now at who you are being because in being is becoming. Drilling down on the vision you hold in your heart – or the whispers of a bigger dream you're not even ready to hold yet – is where *being* turns into *becoming*.

Now you're going to get really intentional about how you step out, what 'fits' and what you believe you were put here to do. Why does that matter? It's all very well having dreams and goals, but if you're not intentional about taking those dreams and using them as blueprints to bring to reality, then they're never going to come to fruition.

As you saw in Part 1, dreams are blueprints for reality, and that bigger vision you've dreamt of is not just in you for Divine entertainment. Blueprints aren't supposed to be the end of the story. The same is true of the vision you've been carrying.

Too often we look around at our circumstances and decide what's possible from that, but when we trust God and press into faith, those limitations are no longer valid, because when God's involved, anything is possible.

So many of us spend time and effort craving proof that we are 'enough'. Even when you've been told for years that you are 'too much' you can, in your heart of hearts feel like you're not enough, not worthy of the dreams on your heart, not worthy of love, of compliments, of nice things.

Many coaches want to help you feel like you are enough and to be fair, in some ways, that's exactly what this book is about. I do, however, want to add a different nuance to what you may be used to – one which I hope will add to what you hear from these other, often fabulous, coaches.

I want to look at the difference between your 'enoughness' as it relates to your worth, and your 'enoughness' for the purpose God put you here to accomplish.

## Innately enough

Your 'enoughness' as a person is innate. You have worth simply by being human. You are as unique as your fingerprint, and utterly irreplaceable. There is NO ONE exactly like you on this planet. None. There never has been, there never will be. YOU are a unique moment in history.

Take a moment to re-read that last bit and take time to meditate on it. Really chew on the idea that you [insert your full name here] are a unique, irreplaceable, never-to-be-repeated moment in history.

What comes up for you as you think about that? Did something in your body baulk at the idea of your uniqueness? Was there a series of 'but, but, but's screaming in your head to reject that idea? Or were you punching the air going 'Heck YES! I am!'

Whether you *feel* like you are uniquely valuable or not does not make it less true that there never has been, nor ever will be someone who is the combination of talents, flaws, experiences, knowledge, beliefs, relationships and so on that make up YOU. Unless you wish to devalue all human life, can you then accept that something/someone this unique has value? Pushing that a little further, can you then play fair with yourself and accept that you too have that value? Your 'enoughness' – in the sense of your worth – was never up for discussion. It is innate. It has never been up for grabs.

## Never intended to be enough

The second type of 'enoughness' often gets mushed in with the first, and that's where things get messy. When you set out to grow your business, you are always going to make mistakes, because you're doing something you've never done before. Learning is done through trial and error. When you were a child, you knew that. You no doubt got into trouble for some of those mistakes, and others you took in your stride. As a child, you were constantly making mistakes, correcting and going again. When you were a baby, no doubt your first forages into feeding yourself resulted in a messy face and all sorts of food in your hair. When you started learning to write, the letters weren't the small, neat letters that you may be capable of now. No, they were huge, sometimes backwards, written on a slant, and probably in crayon... or on a wall. I don't know what scrapes you picked up when you were playing growing up, but I still have a scar on my knee from a harsh lesson in gravity! My friends and I had built a small ramp in the street for us to take our bikes over, and it didn't go to plan for me. Gravity was a mare of a teacher on that occasion!

As a child, and throughout your school years in particular, you had a habit of making mistakes and keeping going. Whether you liked it or not, it was part of learning about the world. As you transition to adulthood, once learning to drive and academic learning are out of the way, it's often the case that your daily exposure to routine failures and readjustments slows down. What can happen then is that failures begin to feel like a bigger deal. You're out of the habit of failing, so now it can feel like failure means something different. I've seen this particularly with clients who have a great fear of failing, not just because they might fail in that instance, but because to fail would also confirm the worst things they believe about themselves. For example, I have had numerous sporting clients who have struggled to aim for international squads because they think that if they fail to qualify for this team, it isn't just that they don't get to compete internationally this year. It also presses on a deeper fear that failure would mean they are 'past it' and too old to chase that bigger dream. This fear of not being 'enough' to *do* something can insidiously become that you *are* not enough, full stop.

As you saw in Part 1, where 'I do' becomes 'I am', you wander into dangerous 'there be dragons' territory. You may want to find your worth in what you do, but what happens when you can't do that anymore? Are you only as 'enough' as you are productive? Lower the stakes and keep your identity well away from any of the roles you have, labels you wear, relationships you're in or work you do. Who you ARE is innately valuable, but for what you were put here to do? Nah, you were never meant to be enough and that is REALLY good news.

# 8:

# 'The unforced rhythms of grace'

*'Are you tired? Worn out? Burned out on religion? Come to me. Get away with me and you'll recover your life. I'll show you how to take a real rest. Walk with me and work with me – watch how I do it. Learn the unforced rhythms of grace. I won't lay anything heavy or ill-fitting on you. Keep company with me and you'll learn to live freely and lightly.'[20]*

I absolutely LOVE this translation of Jesus' words, especially that bit about learning the 'unforced rhythms of grace'. When I first came across this section of Scripture in this translation, it was early 2020, as the Covid-19 pandemic hit, and it lifted me so much. I'd never had a particular love for this section of Scripture. Side note – you're probably getting the picture by now that I have often wrestled with parts of the Bible. I really do. I've had entire rants to God – and others – about sections of Scripture and at other times my Bible is scrawled with notes going 'God, WHAT is this about?' There's so much in those 66 books with all those different genres, and some of what is in there is awful. Absolutely hideous stuff, but then, given that so many of the books detail what happened historically in families, in battles and suchlike, it would be more disturbing if those things had been edited out or glossed over. The Bible doesn't mess about and excuse evil. Even when it's God's own people who are doing it. What Jesus did when He was walking around here was seriously cool. The way He did things that were just NOT the way things worked in that culture was outrageous. Things such as teaching women and defending them, when culturally they were not valued at all as equal with men. Boom. And then there's this bit I've quoted (above) where He's like, 'Chill. Watch and learn kiddo, I've got this'.

This is ridiculous to our self-starter, independent, self-made minds. The idea that you could 'let go and let God' seems outrageous at times, even to Christians. We all live in a world that idolises productivity, that worships the wealthy and applauds those who work insane amounts of hours as if that were the point of living. Scratch the surface and you'll find more than a few of those hustlers are doing it to try and feel like they're enough. I know because I used to be one of them.

Here's Jesus offering you a completely different pace. He's not offering to teach you how to sprint harder, work more, be more productive. He's offering you rest. He's offering to make it easy. That is mind-blowing when you've been taught that it's all about how hard you can work. When you've been encouraged by others who're impressed at the long hours you put in and how much you've sacrificed, it's outrageous, if not galling, for this punk Jesus to come along and tell you that this can feel chilled and easy, instead of fraught with struggles and exhausting.

Can you even contemplate that? My former striving self was a queen of burnout and always felt 'lazy'. No matter how hard I worked I could never feel like it was enough, like I was enough and if Jesus had stood in front of me and said that stuff about rest, I would've wanted to roar in His face. That version of me would've been like 'Don't you see? I don't have TIME to rest!' She'd have completely missed the point. Yet the version of me that God was reaching with this translation in 2020 was one who decided early in the pandemic to reduce her hours strategically so that I could protect my own energy in order to better serve my clients.

## You're not broken or defective

I know how it feels to look at people who seem to achieve so much and feel less than in comparison to them. Their work rate seems so much more than yours. Their achievements so much more impressive. And yet, so what?

You are so precious. Your worth cannot be removed from you. You are uniquely loved. That doesn't mean God loves us equally, but rather you are dearly cherished and delighted in for who God sees that you are and can be, without reference to anyone else. You were not designed to be ranked alongside anyone else, and the love God has for you is not just some scraps left over after He's finished loving everyone else. Nope. You are uniquely loved. Uniquely created. Uniquely purposed. You may be different but that is not a bug in the system. You are different by design. The world may not understand you, heck, you may not understand you, but there is meaning to you being you.

You weren't meant to be 'them', or you would... be them. You are you. So take away that false comparison and sense of pressure to be 'enough'. I say that because if you don't understand your worth, no amount of recognition, no awards and accolades, no title nor size of bank account will fill the aching gap in your soul. None. So, give up that fight and let's see if you can't begin to grasp the wonder that you are and the life God intended to gift you with.

Megan Foster, founder of Fostering Excellence says:

'[When] I started working with Dr Kathrine... [my] life was 90 percent hustle and 10 percent brainstorming more ways to hustle, and I was burning out fast. Time off, vacations, and relaxing were not in my vocabulary, much less actionable. Fast forward to [now], I have the work-life balance that is functional, sustainable, and motivating me to give more to my industry in ways that I only dreamt about before. I take time off, I spend more time with my family, and I genuinely enjoy my work more than ever before.

Dr Kathrine helped me take back the most precious resource any of us has: time.'

## Never intended to do this alone

When you think about who you were created to be and what burns in your heart to do, it's supposed to be light. God is not about weighing you down, so if the burden you're carrying is heavy, you're carrying too much of it. That was never God's plan, so have a look at where you're trying to accomplish everything in your own strength.

I'm not saying that you can't accomplish incredible things in your own strength – of course you can. I'm just saying that you're making things harder than they need to be.

You were never intended to do any of this alone, and I'm not just talking about God here. We are created for relationship. We *need* each other. All of us need people who can speak wisdom to us, hold us accountable, encourage us, guide us, teach us, and perhaps even help us to stop and take a rest. We all need the assistance of others, whether it's the mentor who helps you level up or the mechanic who keeps your car on the road. It's not weak to accept help. It's how you go further faster. You can be stubborn, proud and independent all you like on this point – Lord knows I certainly have – but somewhere along the lines, you'll either make unnecessary mistakes because you didn't allow others to help you, or you'll make yourself ill. Learn to receive help.

It's not just the receiving though in which we're designed to need each other. The opposite is also true. I know that for many of us who've ever struggled to feel like we're enough, being taught that you are enough is nice but it can take a while to land. Sometimes, being shown how you need to get the memo for others' sake is a quicker route to grasping the importance of walking in your enoughness and purpose. In this next chapter I am going to dive more deeply into a universal principle that I trust will help you if you're big-hearted towards others but have been struggling to feel your own worth.

# 9:

## The parable of the
## *Irregular Choice* shoes

THERE is a parable in the Bible that I really used to hate. Just keeping it real. I never want you to think that I'm just drinking Kool-Aid without wrestling with it. I will always encourage you to do the same with anything anyone teaches you. Think on it, check it out, wrestle with what you're learning. If it's truth, it can stand up to rigorous questioning. And honestly? If this God I believe in were too fragile to handle my questions, He'd be absolutely no use for helping me with the bigger messes I've made along the way. He's more than able to handle my screw ups, and my wrangling with the bits I don't understand. This particular passage I struggled with is called the 'Parable of the Talents' (find it in Matthew 25:14–30) and in the *New Living Translation* it goes like this:

*[14] Again, the Kingdom of Heaven can be illustrated by the story of a man going on a long trip. He called together his servants and entrusted his money to them while he was gone. [15] He gave five bags of silver to one, two bags of silver to another, and one bag of silver to the last – dividing it in proportion to their abilities. He then left on his trip. [16] The servant who received the five bags of silver began to invest*

the money and earned five more. <sup>17</sup> The servant with two bags of silver also went to work and earned two more. <sup>18</sup> But the servant who received the one bag of silver dug a hole in the ground and hid the master's money.

<sup>19</sup> After a long time their master returned from his trip and called them to give an account of how they had used his money. <sup>20</sup> The servant to whom he had entrusted the five bags of silver came forward with five more and said, 'Master, you gave me five bags of silver to invest, and I have earned five more.'

<sup>21</sup> The master was full of praise. 'Well done, my good and faithful servant. You have been faithful in handling this small amount, so now I will give you many more responsibilities. Let's celebrate together!'

<sup>22</sup> The servant who had received the two bags of silver came forward and said, 'Master, you gave me two bags of silver to invest, and I have earned two more.' <sup>23</sup> The master said, 'Well done, my good and faithful servant. You have been faithful in handling this small amount, so now I will give you many more responsibilities. Let's celebrate together!'

<sup>24</sup> Then the servant with the one bag of silver came and said, 'Master, I knew you were a harsh man, harvesting crops you didn't plant and gathering crops you didn't cultivate. <sup>25</sup> I was afraid I would lose your money, so I hid it in the earth. Look, here is your money back.'

<sup>26</sup> But the master replied, 'You wicked and lazy servant! If you knew I harvested crops I didn't plant and gathered crops I didn't cultivate, <sup>27</sup> why didn't you deposit my money in the bank? At least I could have gotten some interest on it.'

<sup>28</sup> Then he ordered, 'Take the money from this servant, and give it to the one with the ten bags of silver. <sup>29</sup> To those who use well what they are given, even more will be given, and they will have an abundance. But from those who do nothing, even what little they have will be taken away. <sup>30</sup> Now throw

*this useless servant into outer darkness, where there will be*
*weeping and gnashing of teeth.'*

I don't know how this hits you, but growing up it really used to gall me that the guy with the most got more and the poor numpty with one talent had even that taken off him.

Obviously, I was wrong. That's not the point. To demonstrate the point in a way that makes sense even to me, I want to make it using shoes. Specifically, to *Irregular Choice* shoes[21]. Look them up and you'll find all sorts of fabulous designs... and a bunch of absolutely bonkers ones! I love nice shoes, so let me tell you how I used fabulous footwear to make sense of this parable.

Picture the scene. I gather three of my team and present them each with shoes. For one member of my team, I've selected five pairs of amazing *Irregular Choice* shoes especially for them. I've chosen ones I know they'd enjoy wearing, that they'd look good in, and that would be more perfect for them than for anyone else on my team. (I realise I'm stretching the text of the parable here, but I don't believe that I am stepping beyond the spirit of it, so humour me on this!)

I've selected two pairs for my next team member, and the third I've selected one pair for. I don't want to put too much pressure on anyone, so the team member who gets five pairs is someone I know can work those five pairs without feeling overwhelmed. I've carefully considered each of their abilities, the events they have coming up on the calendar that I already know about, and I have gifted them accordingly.

Then off I go on holiday, leaving my team to use the shoes as best they can.

When I come back, I find that the first team member has rocked their shoes. She's put those babies to work! The second team member has put theirs on, broken them in and made the most of them too. But the third team member has taken their pair and hidden them in the back of the closet, for fear of getting a mark on them or wearing them wrong!

I am so excited when I hear how the first and second team members have rocked their shoes – how they've tried them with different outfits, how much fun others have got from seeing them too, and how they've inspired others to wear their own fabulous shoes.

OK so there may have been a few fashion *faux pas*, and there are marks on the shoes, but they've been loved and worn, and heck, they're shoes! I knew when I gave the first team member her shoes that she was a mud magnet and could trip over her own shadow. I'd factored that into the choice of shoes I gave her, and I don't care about the marks because she got and gave pleasure with what I gave her, and that's great.

The third team member though. Well, I'm not happy with them at all. I gave her something that would be good for her, that would have felt good to wear, but she didn't try them on! She hid them in a closet so not only did she rob herself of the joy they'd have brought her, but she also robbed everyone else too! I'd take those shoes back – I'm not having them go to waste when there are other people who need to see them and benefit from them! I'll give them to the team member with five pairs, because I know they can be trusted to put them to use!

When she started to make excuses, I can imagine myself saying 'What do you mean you were scared to get any marks on them? I *know* you, I hired you, and I know there's mud out there. None of that is a surprise to me! I factored that in. I just wanted you to use what you had. You come asking me for more, but you've not even used what you already had, so why would I waste more on you?'

And there it is. Now I get why the talent was taken from the third servant and given to the first.

It's not that the boss doesn't want to bless the third servant, but rather that the third servant let fear, laziness and excuses of who knows what flavour to hold him back and prevent him from doing good with what he had.

He failed by default. His inertia was his undoing. Fear cost him more than merely what he could have gained: it also cost him what he already had.

And then he didn't even take responsibility for his actions but tried to blame his fears on the boss. Top tip: blaming your boss for your actions will not end well.

So why am I sharing this with you? You didn't sign up for Bible study so what, pray tell, is the point?

I'm glad you asked. There are several important points I want you to hear from this story.

## Haves and have nots

How often are we so concerned with what we haven't got or how much more others have, that we fail to acknowledge and use what we HAVE got?

It's so easy to be tripped up in comparison or to hear the imposter gremlin telling you that that person has so much more ability than you... and look how that gremlin implies that this means THEY should do the important things, because they're so much better at them than you are. But if only the best ever do things, there's going to be a heck of a lot of burned out 'greats' and a heck of a lot of good that doesn't get done.

Comparison is a distraction. It can be a convincing excuse, but it doesn't make the world a better place. It's also false because you are unique. Who should you be compared to? Do you see how your belief about your enoughness is crucial? FORGET anyone else. What have you been given? How are you going to use that? Perfection is not required.

## Use it or lose it

Like muscles, if you don't use your talents, you will lose them. It's that simple. If you're not working on your fitness, you know that the fitness you had when you were working out is going to diminish. If you learn to be fluent in a language and then never use those language skills, your fluency will drop and you'll forget words, tenses and phrases that you once knew.

Paradoxically, if you work on your language skills and continue to practise them, guess what? You'll develop MORE. If you work on your fitness, you'll increase your muscle strength, your endurance and your flexibility.

This principle is unavoidable, and it applies whether you want it to or not. It also applies to your comfort zone. If you only do things that feel easy and don't require risk or effort, like the third servant, good things will not come from that. The reward of comfort is comfort. That's it. And even at that, I'd say it's not really a reward!

If you want to have impact in your world and you want to get braver in standing up and being fully who God created you to be, then you will have to step out and grow. You will have to do the 'reps' that you don't think you're strong enough to do – and you will likely think that because you haven't done them yet.

You're going to have to practise the things that make your brain hurt, because learning to navigate the world in a new way means going beyond what is familiar, what you know, and stepping out into new territory. This will require risking failures.


## God has factored in your screw ups

I know from personal experience that perfectionism is a cruel master. It is relentless and never satisfied. It is always moving the goalposts. When you fear making a mistake that you'll be held accountable for, beware. That fear can paralyse you from acting, and then you fail by default, through inaction.

Where God is concerned, you were lovingly designed and given gifts and abilities – some of which you may not even have discovered yet!

But God is not delusional. Your capacity for mistakes or self-preservation does not come as a surprise to God! God is not watching going, 'Well, I didn't see that coming!!' There's not a gasp in heaven and God shaking His head going, 'Well, if I'd known they were going to do THAT, I'd never have given them this talent!'

It's not that God wants you to fail, and certainly not that Jesus takes delight in it or anything like that. No. Rather, it is not the end of your story. God always has redemption available for you, no matter how spectacularly you mess up.

If you're afraid of screwing up what God gave you and fear wrath for the mess you make, then I want to encourage you to dig deep into the Bible and read how adored you are, how desperately God is rooting for you and how relentlessly He pursues relationship with you. You are LOVED. God roots for you.

## Your gifts are not accidental

I honestly believe that you were carefully and thoughtfully created. I don't believe it's an accident that you were given the gifts and talents that you have, and I also want to encourage you that although they are given TO you, they are not just FOR you, but to bless others THROUGH you. Does that mean that they won't be a joy to you? Of course not, they absolutely can be and regularly are.

However, your abilities are not just for you. They are not something that affects only you if you don't use them. If you do not use your gifts, other people lose out on their benefits too. If you don't write that book you've been dreaming of because you're afraid of what people will think of it, you rob your potential readers of the experience they would have had in your book.

Incidentally, that experience is only partly down to the words you put on the page, it is also due to the magic that happens when someone reads those words, and their brain makes its own connections from them! I will say that some of the books that have had the biggest impact on me have been ones that I really wrestled with, because they made me think in new ways, to better understand my convictions, or to gain new perspectives on issues I thought I had previously understood well.

## Fear destroys lives

I have already alluded to it above, but I want to encourage you that fear is a liar. It will rob you of your dreams and leave you with a small life. It will catastrophise and give you any number of reasons why your dreams are stupid, impossible, impossible for *you*, not the right time, or better suited for someone else.

There are so many downright lies that fear will tell you in its craven desire to feel 'safe'. That desire to stay safe had the third servant in the story playing small – if we can say that he was 'playing' at all! It led to more fear, a smaller existence and the contempt of his boss. It ultimately led to the very circumstances he was trying to protect himself from. Because that is the ultimate lie fear tells. Fear says that if you do what I say, you'll be safe.

That is a lie.

It can offer you no guarantees, only familiarity.

It can offer you no dreams, only 'what if's.

It can offer you no security, just the myth of it.

What fear actually does is make failure and loss certain.

Perhaps not in as dramatic or public a way as if you tried and failed, but you will certainly feel the sting of failure... corrosive avoidance, by corrosive avoidance.

I KNOW fear can sound logical. I heard it every time it wanted to stop me sitting down to write this book! But like you, I need to accept that fear is having its own panic attack and trying to control what I do, so that I stick with what is familiar. I visualise myself soothing it, telling fear that I've got this and it's going to be OK. Tell fear to have a cookie, and then rattle on regardless.

That maybe sounds crazy, but honouring that fear is trying to keep you safe can give you enough wriggle room to acknowledge the feeling and move past it. Visualising fear as a younger version of yourself can remind you that you are growing and taking responsibility for your life, and there is something that feels empowering in doing that. Whether you are partnering with God or not, you need to be an active participant in your one fabulous life! There is no shame in feeling fear. We *all* face it, and it is a good thing for those times when it really will keep you safe! However, when it is what constantly drives your actions, it has become a problem, a petulant mental gremlin that needs a time out!

---

## OVER TO YOU

- How might you picture fear as a person/creature? Don't picture it as yourself, imagine it is a being that is completely separate from you, someone or something you can have a conversation with.
- What does fear often say to you?
- If fear were a person standing in front of you, what does it often say to get you to do what it wants?
- What does it say will happen if you ignore it?
- What effects does that have on you?

- When fear gets the better of you, how do you feel? What do you think about?
- When has fear kept you back from doing something you wanted to do?
- Does it impact how you see yourself or your skills?
- How do you feel about the effects fear has on you?
- What would you like to say or do when fear starts trying to control you? Let's get really practical and show fear up for the limiter that it is.
- What would you do if fear wasn't standing in your way? List specific actions you'd take, and ways that you might be doing the same things in a different way. Be very specific!
- How will you show up in your world differently when fear isn't controlling your actions?
- Now let's think about how you'll BE different. For example, will you put yourself forward more, rather than trying to be invisible? Will you be an encourager to others, rather than being afraid to say anything in case someone takes it the wrong way? Maybe you'll no longer be the one that is quick to be sarcastic and cynical, instead being the first to build up and congratulate. How will you show up differently in your energy, in your outlook, in how you engage with others?
- What is to stop you taking a step today to experience yourself now as the person who takes those actions?

## 10:

## To everything there is a season...

A S I stated right back at the start of this book, you were created to be here at this specific time in history. Assuming you are not a Divine burp and are in fact here by design rather than an Almighty 'oops', why did God place you here at *this* moment in history? Why did your world need you in it *now*?

The fact you're still here speaks to purpose, speaks to you not being done yet. So what is undone? You might not know, but this is the time to start dreaming, start pressing in and asking God what is lined up that you can be doing to use your talents for the benefit of others.

You have unique gifts and purpose. You are a unique cocktail of skills, experiences and indeed flaws. You were born into a particular geographical context, with its own nuances, norms and expectations, and the path you have trodden so far gives you a unique outlook on the world. The way that you can speak to issues, and the stories you can call on are distinct from others and will help people because they resonate in just the right way. You can identify with the people God has for you to help. You can relate to them where others simply cannot, no matter how much they wish to.

If you're an introvert, for example, you understand that other introverts not wanting to attend a big party, but being perfectly happy to meet up with just a couple of people, is not them being stand-offish or antisocial. It's actually them being social their way and it better fits what is energising for them. When I talk about introvert/extrovert in this way, I mean how you recharge your batteries. I'm not talking about how loud you are or how confident you are to stand up in front of a crowd. I'm certainly happy to be the centre of attention and love speaking engagements. I love a stage and am more than happy to do off the cuff Q&A on topics I'm knowledgeable about. HOWEVER. I recharge by being alone or with one or two people I am close to. Crowds and big groups take energy from me. My sister, Jenny, is very different. She is an absolute extrovert in how she re-energises. She throws fantastic parties and has a large group of friends... the group energy is like plugging her in to a rapid charger. For me, though, after the first wee while of being sociable, I'll be the one in the kitchen doing something useful and having a meaty conversation with someone. It's important to know what lights you up and how you recharge, so that you can protect your energy and not end up drained by either too much time away from people, or too much time with them!

## If she can, you can

Julie is one of my dog sport competitor clients. When we first began working together, she was working towards winning at national level with a hope of competing internationally. One reason she was doubting her ability to take things to the International stage was that she found Nationals really tough. There were always multiple rings, thousands of competitors and a lot of noise at her country's Nationals and it all took place over several days. Never mind how big the venue was and all the extra things she had to navigate to even get there, such as flights. It was a lot to take in, and certainly far, far more than she was used to on a day-to-day basis. A lot of her friends would also be there: some of them as competitors and others there to spectate and enjoy the experience, so she felt a lot of pressure to spend time with them too. She told me that she'd get more and more tired as the event went on and by the final day, she was a mere shadow of her former self.

One thing I know about people who compete in dog agility: many, many of them are introverts. It doesn't matter what country they're from or at what level they compete, more times than not, when I run surveys about how they prefer to recharge, they will describe introverted scenarios. Julie was no different. Put in a group, she'd often take herself off where she could be alone with her thoughts and focus on the run she was about to do. Putting this competitor in a busy environment where she was constantly surrounded by people and having to interact, was tiring. So, as we prepared for her next Nationals, we planned in ways that she could intentionally get rest and quiet times. We planned to work WITH her, not trying to make her like anybody else, but with what made sense for HER. She created routines and plans. She had planned lines to excuse herself if she needed time out, we covered all eventualities like a rash! You name it, we had it covered. Our plans worked, and she has since medalled multiple times internationally and represented her country at world level.

## Quit 'should'-ing yourself

You were put here at this point in time to be different by definition. Remember that you are utterly unique, so OF COURSE there are going to be unique ways that you want to show up or run your business. That's the way it should be, but it can be tough when us humans like to categorise things, to step outside the existing boxes and 'ways things are done'. You wouldn't be reading this book though if some part of you didn't look at some of the 'shoulds' you're taught and feel uncomfortable with them. You feel some of them are inauthentic for you but transgressing what the experts say in all those courses can be difficult. They've apparently earned millions, so who are you to question them?

Who you are is you. That utterly loved, uniquely-fleshed and innately-enough spirit who looks back at you from the mirror. The one who has your values, who craves to help the people you love to serve, in the accept-no-substitutes authentic way that only you can. Not only *can* you question what you've been taught, if it doesn't 'fit' who you are, how you're wired, and what matters most to you, then I say you *must* question it. What if you were put here at this time to pioneer a better way forward that doesn't just liberate you from icky ways of working, but that liberates thousands and creates a paradigm shift in your industry? If that little voice wants to laugh at the idea of you being a pioneer, let me remind you that you can tell it to sit down and shut its cake hole. Oh, and while I'm at it, why NOT you?

Julie would've continued to struggle if she had tried to do things as others do. Thankfully she took time to work out what made sense for *her*, regardless of whether anyone else did things that way. Don't you think that other introverts will have seen what she did? Do you not think she opened a way for others to copy her behaviours and protect their own energy? Of course she did. Even if it was only in her immediate friendship group, her daring to do what made sense for her brought liberation and fresh opportunities for others too.

If you are not doing you as only you can do – or if you're too busy trying to squish yourself ugly-sister style into someone else's way of doing things, then it will wear you out and the people who would have been helped by seeing how you are different will miss out. If you don't model your difference for them, they cannot learn from you what that looks like.

## OVER TO YOU

- What about you? Where do the 'shoulds' not fit you?
- Where do you find yourself feeling uncomfortable about what you're being taught?
- How do you need to do things differently than others? Even if you don't yet know *how* you want to do things 'your' way, knowing what doesn't fit you is a great place to start.

# 11:

## Rhythmic, not monotonously consistent

A S you may have guessed from my 'garden' analogy in chapter two of this book, I love gardening. No, that's not quite right. I love growing fruit and vegetables. I'm starting to do the flower growing thing, but basically I am predominantly interested in something that grows and yields food. That's magic to me, and I love it.

When I was a child, I started with herbs and grew all manner of them. Everything from chives and multiple varieties of mint (word to the wise: you've got to grow mint in containers so it doesn't take over everything), marjoram, rosemary, thyme, curry plant, oregano, parsley, sage – you name it, I was cluttering up our back garden with it!

I moved on to tomatoes and strawberries next when I lived in the south of England. They grew brilliantly and were thoroughly and comprehensively enjoyed by the local deer if not also the squirrels. For all that it was a bummer not to get to personally enjoy the fruits of my labours, I could never quite bring myself to begrudge having deer and goodness knows what else wandering about my garden.

Fast forward and now, every year, I plant a bunch of stuff, still with negligible expertise. Remarkably, things grow. That's one thing about fruit and veg that I love: most of them have a decent will to live. They'll also get on with the business of growing with minimal fuss or interference from me. Of course, I also plant like a five-year-old in that, once I plant something, I am impatiently willing there to be a harvest within a week. But that's not how nature works.

Despite what many of the gurus would have you believe, we humans are not 'consistent' all the time. People, like my plants, have seasons to our lives. Like the rest of nature, we are cyclical and rhythmic. I realise that this may sound anathema to you, especially if you are well versed in the social media expert's credo that you must be 'consistent'. And sure, to satisfy an algorithm, they have a point.

HOWEVER.

You were not created to satisfy the whims of tech companies or their algorithms. A satisfying and richly-full life is not one that dances to the tune of a tech company, no matter how much money it may bring you. That may bring you a busy-full life, but it's not what God had in mind for you. As we saw earlier, Jesus wasn't exhorting you to do more, but offering to show you how to take an honest-to-goodness rest. He's not going to force you. He knows the pace that is healthy for your body and your life but God created consent so whilst you may reap the burnout consequences of refusing to rest, He is never going to force you to quit hustling beyond what is healthy for you. Your own body-breaking pace can do that it on its own though, so you can either take rest intentionally now, or your body will down tools at a time of its choosing. I can say that with great authority since I didn't learn that lesson the easy way... or the first time around!

## Seasonal trends

When my niece Karis was about four, she and her family were over visiting my parents from Scotland. My parents have a dog training centre on a beautiful piece of land with a river and all sorts of trees along the riverbank. It was November and my dad showed Karis a young pear tree that he had recently planted. He told her that next time she visited there would be pears on it and she could pick them! At the time, this was a fun thing to say since he didn't expect Karis to be back across until there would indeed be pears on the tree. She came back in March, though, and was of course too young to understand about how fruit grows on trees or seasons or any of that.

My dad, ever the doting grandpa, could not let her be disappointed, so off he went to the supermarket where he bought pears and tied them one by one to the tree with string so that she would have pears to pick, just as he had promised. Karis duly came along to pick the pears and we have a photograph of pure glee as this wee scrap of a thing proudly holds up the shopping bag of pears that she had 'picked' from grandpa's tree! It was apparently so much fun that she asked grandpa if there'd be more pears to pick if she came back the next week!

## Ebb and flow

Just as plants take time to grow in one season, there are also seasons for flourishing and seasons for hibernation. One thing that grates on me about the hustle culture that worships consistency on the altar of algorithms is that it does not allow for ebb and flow. If you've ever met a human, you know that we're really not that great at being consistent. No matter how much you want something, expecting that you'll be able to forge ahead with the same energy and enthusiasm every day of every season without end is, to use the technical term, bonkers.

And the great news about this, is that you already know that life has rhythms. Sometimes it's the hormonal rhythms throughout the month, and how your energy, moods, and pain levels may vary. Sometimes it's that you're solar powered, so the sunnier months of the year are those in which you revel and you suddenly find yourself with an increased energy to get things done. Perhaps for you, your rhythms are set around others: your children's academic year or your husband's military deployments. These are all relatively short-term rhythmic changes that you may face, but there are bigger rhythms too.

Imagine the stereotypical life trajectory of a woman in contemporary society. As a girl, in a democratic society, she expects to go to school alongside boys and – theoretically at least – be able to pursue school studies to university level if she so chooses. After leaving school or university, the traditional trajectory will include expectations that she gets a job, gets married, buys a house, has children... looks after them (with or without job/s depending on economic privilege to choose), helps them grow until they leave the nest, goes through the menopause... and so on.

Whether you agree with this stereotype or not is beside the point. I recognise that it can be profoundly different depending on privilege. You may have faced a different timeline placed before you. Perhaps you eschewed the timeline others had for you. What matters is that life has seasons which we might very roughly define as: child, teenage years, young adulthood, middle age, old age. The things that are expected in each season – rightly or wrongly – also influence the rhythms of life. Yet when it comes to business, this natural fluctuation is not reflected let alone honoured in much that is taught. I believe that omission is damaging.

If you're in a season of raising children, for example, your vision – at least, the one God has for you – includes those children you are caring for. Those you are caring for are not a distraction from your vision, they are part of it! They're not an impediment to your purpose, they are an essential strand of it. You're not lacking in motivation if you cannot dedicate all your time to your business because you have parents who're frail and need support, or a teen navigating the hormonal delights of adolescence who needs your attention. Your vision, mission, purpose as God intended honours all those things because they are part of your life *in this season*. Things will change as seasons change but understand that the life you have outside your money-making activities is not less important or proof that you're not dedicated enough. It's just been treated that way by a deficient understanding of what life is about and how utterly rich it can be, in ways that cannot be solely quantified on a balance sheet.

---

## OVER TO YOU

- What season are you in?
- Who do you need to care for or prioritise?
- What is a healthy rhythm to life and work that honours the season you're in?

---

### Life on different timelines

Did you know? Hazelnut trees can produce nuts when they're just two years old, and certainly should by the time they're five. On the other hand, the oak does not mature enough to produce acorns until it's roughly 20 years old and doesn't reach peak acorn production until it's around 50 years old.

Two different trees, two very different trajectories. They're MEANT to be different. The hazelnut is not better because it fruits quicker. The oak is not behind or deficient because it takes longer.

**BIG** IDEA: Don't judge your progress by someone else's timeline. Life is for living, not striving and beating yourself up that you're not going at the same rate as anyone else. Enjoy the journey and everything that you're learning as you grow along.

The longevity of the hazel tree is expected to be 70–80 years (without heavy coppicing to help it live longer). The oak tree can live for a thousand years, though a mere 600 years is apparently more typically expected.

In order to grow to maturity in such a way that it can live for hundreds of years, the oak takes longer to mature. Who's to say you're not the same? When you're out in a forest, you might find trees that you're particularly drawn to, but it's likely that you don't waste time comparing one variety of tree to another and finding one wanting. I doubt you stand in front of an oak tree and shame it for not having copious acorns on it, or tell it that if it was any good, it would be like the hazel over there which is loaded with hazelnuts and feeding entire families of squirrels. Of course, you wouldn't do that. That would be weird. Yet I bet you've compared yourself to someone else who's already achieved what you want – and decided that you didn't match up.

You're not doing things at 'their' speed, because you are not them. You can absolutely continue to burn yourself out trying to match up to someone else, but if you do that, you'll miss out on the adventure of being you.

## You're not behind

I completely get how frustrating it feels to look at others apparently zooming past you and to feel like you're behind, but you're not them. Not all plants that sprout up quickly are healthy. Sometimes a plant gets too much sun, or soil that's too rich and it shoots up, looking all healthy, but then you find that it has barely any roots and when the first decent gust of wind comes, boom, there it goes, crashing down. It's also tempting to look at someone who's been 'quickly' successful and feel behind. What this pre-supposes though is that you know the whole story of how they got there, which most of the time you don't!

You don't know how many failures they've endured in the past, or how many false starts it's taken to get to this point. And frankly, even if it's zero, their trajectory is none of your concern.

Of course, the flip side of that is feeling guilty that you're so much further on or like you've had it so much easier than others. There's something I see often with my successful clients who've come up from modest beginnings. It's almost a survivor's guilt. They often feel bad that they can afford nice things and like they shouldn't show pictures of their vacations or adventures, because others don't have what they have. There will always be people in front of you and people behind you, and at some point, you need to reconcile yourself with that fact, without pride at those you are ahead of or shame at those you perceive yourself to be behind. Quit looking at others for reasons why you're not enough. Or too much. This is where you are, and it's up to you what you do with that.

## OVER TO YOU

- Where do you feel pressure to move at a different pace?
- Where do you feel like you're behind?
- If you were able to work at your pace, what would your day look like?
- What would the rhythm of your year look like?
- When in the day are you most energised or most focused?
- How can you schedule your day to make the most of the time when you feel most energised?

# 12:

## Money

THE drive to be relentlessly consistent feeds the cultural message that we need to be productive. This way of thinking privileges the time when we are productive (often meaning 'earning money') over activities which are not explicitly productive. So time with family is 'unproductive', time off is 'unproductive', hobbies are 'unproductive'. You may think that you don't subscribe to this way of thinking and maybe you genuinely don't agree with it, but how often have you felt guilty for not doing what you 'should' be, in favour of something fun? Now let's look at this money connection and dig a little deeper into it.

### Money as god

We live in a world where money is worshipped. Those who have it are lauded and there is a sort of halo effect where their wealth implies that their knowledge is superior to those with less. They are perceived as being 'better', more 'successful' and their opinions and endorsement as having more weight.

Rubbish.

The business world, not least the online business world that I know so well, is full of messages about how you should always be aiming to earn more, to have a bigger launch next time. I find myself asking WHY?

This pre-supposes that more money is always the goal. *To what end?* Is that really all that life is about? Is money really all that matters? And don't go telling me that 'when you make more you can give more'. Technically that's true, but in reality, there's a powerful lot of good you can do in the world around you without being rich too.

Arguably, the trade-off for earning so much more to help people out there somewhere is that you're potentially less present and invested in the people closest to you, the loved ones you were first entrusted with nurturing and guiding. This relentless, insatiable quest for more ultimately demands a 'yes' which means, by definition, that you are saying 'no' to something else somewhere along the lines. What are you currently saying 'yes' to and what do those 'yes'es result in you saying 'no' to? Does this fit with what matters most in your life and where you dream of going?

If money is the end goal in itself, it leads to absolute poverty. Oh, the bank account might fill up nicely, but if money is being gathered for money's sake, then it is little more than an idol and it is going to shrivel the soul of the person gaining it.

I am quite sure you do not need me to give you names of people who exemplify this trait. They have more money than they know what to do with, and, instead of using it to make a difference in the lives of others, they hoard it. Or they spend it on things that DO. NOT. MATTER.

Now, you might take issue with this. You might be sucking in your breath thinking that I'm trying to promote some sort of communist utopia. Nope. Absolutely not. Communism doesn't work, not least because of, uh, humans. That's not where I'm going with this at all. I'm certainly not saying that money is bad or that making a lot of money is bad. Nope. If you're called to business, then you're called to, at the very least, make more money than you spend! Money is just a tool, so I'm NOT saying anything about money in and of itself.

I AM saying that when you focus on the number in your bank account as the be-all and end-all, it is very easy to look down on those who have less than you, to suggest that you are more important (more 'enough') than them, to decry sharing your wealth as a 'handout' to those who 'don't work as hard' as you, or to otherwise make excuses for why you simply can't share from your overflowing pot to make the world a better place.

We exist at the minute in the midst of a consumptive template of how to do business. It thrives on our dissatisfaction and endless quest for more. Unlike nature, it consumes, rather than grows and regenerates, so its attitude to money is problematic in many ways. The attitude is so widespread – all you have to do is go into a business group on Facebook and tell them that you're perfectly happy with where you're at and say that you actually don't want to earn any more money... and watch how people recoil and scatter from you like cockroaches from light. You'll have any amount of coaches offering to help you work through your 'mindset' issues, clear your 'money blocks' and goodness knows what else. What is missed is that you were merely expressing that you've reached your 'enough' and are content. THAT is how broken this business model is for real human lives.

## Money as a tool

If money by itself is not a good goal, should you put a personal cap on what you earn?

Money is a tool. Not a god. Not a fix-all. As has been seen in times of financial crash, it is not the security blanket that we'd like to tell ourselves that it is. Money will not make you more secure. I'm going to throw in there though that I know a God who can offer you security if you will let Him. Money is a tool, and the way that you choose to use it shows where your priorities and heart are. If increasing wealth does not result in positive impact on the world around you, is that an intentional choice not to use your wealth to help others or a fear that it will disappear again? Is it a moral deadening that needs to be lifted so you can reconnect to the world around you, even if that feels scary and will most likely be a bit on the messy side?

How does it feel to think of what you have as being 'blessed to be a blessing'? I encourage you to sit with this thought this week. Imagine how your resources could make a difference to the world around you, directly or indirectly. Money may not be sent directly by giving to a cause you support, but perhaps your wealth allows you free time to volunteer somewhere, perhaps offering your skills to a community group. A fabulous friend of mine, Olwen, is a retired maths teacher and school principal. She gives her time for free to teach adults maths so they can get their GCSE[22] qualification and improve their employment prospects. What do you have to offer others that you can share from your resources and make your world a better place?

## Wealth is not shameful and there is dignity in work

Whether you are as broke as the proverbial church mouse, or absolutely rolling in money, I am not shaming you. I am certainly not suggesting that poverty is more virtuous than wealth. Not at all. That particular lie from the pit of hell held me back for years, so if it has held you back, let me kill it right here and now.

There are incredible people who are wealthy and use their wealth not just for selfish means, but as a tool to make the world a better place. And there are poor people who hoard, covet and do harm with the little they have by way of financial resources. It's not the number in the account that is the differentiator. Money doesn't make character, it reveals it.

Similarly, there is dignity in work. We can probably all think of a time when we were able to buy a first present for someone we loved, or able to buy a meal with family, or some other formative moment where, for the first time, you felt able to contribute from what you earned. Similarly, you may know someone who has been out of work for a while despite their best efforts, or perhaps that has been you, and you have felt how soul-destroying it can be not to be working and able to contribute. This is why I say there is dignity in work. It's not about drudgery, but a gift, and at some level we get that. It's why it can feel so rotten when you can't work for some reason, for example through ill health (and I've been there too). Of course, there are other factors and I don't mean to over-simplify, but my point is that work is good. Being able to provide for your and your family's needs is good. Being able to provide for others is good. There are always going to be many – locally, nationally, and globally – who cannot work or cannot support themselves even as they work. There are many who are vulnerable, many who need rescuing from all manner of living hells, so many who need protection, restoration, intervention, support and dignity. When we get to be part of restoring their dignity and helping those people be safe and secure, that is something incredible, and it is a gift available to us. Note though, that it is in situations like this where the vital difference between innate 'enough'-ness and 'enough'-ness for tasks is so important to extrapolate. Someone who cannot work is as innately priceless and enough as someone who is able to be wildly productive. That's not the message that is sometimes conveyed in society, but I believe it is an important truth. If we lose sight of the innate priceless value of a person, we are in grave danger of thinking, speaking and acting in ways that are harmful to that person or group of people. Since we are all human and susceptible to illness, treating people who are down on their luck as less-than or other is a risky business as any of us are only ever some circumstances away from finding ourselves in similar predicaments. In summary, treat others as having the worth that you'd like to be understood to have!

## The heart behind the balance sheet

It is not the number in the account that is the point here. WHY do you want to earn more? There are many very valid reasons why you need or want to earn more. My point in talking about money specifically is because what you think of it and the importance you give it will determine whether you or it call the shots.

If you think having more money will tell you anything about yourself, I want to urge you to beware. Money is not a good way to determine your identity. The world may do that but it will be soul-destroying for you if you buy into the idea that wealth means worth. You are irreplaceable. There is something wrong if money is the sole benchmark for impact and success. Don't buy into the lie that money/celebrity is synonymous with expertise. That's a halo effect that can be utter nonsense. And don't buy into any whisper that tries to tell you that if you could only earn six-, seven-, eight-figures, or a following of [pick a number] *then* you'd feel enough. Just like trying to find your identity in your work, believing you can find your worth and identity if you just earn more is similarly fruitless.

## OVER TO YOU

- If you want to earn more, why? What is the end goal, the purpose of the money in your bank account?
- Consider what motivates you to want more and whether it's just what you've been told to want.
- How will you know what is 'enough' for you?
- Where is the line at which point the 'yes' would rob you and have you say 'no' to something precious?
- What matters more to you than how much money you have?
- What will you NOT sacrifice in order to earn more?
- Be honest, how might your identity be affected if you were to stop striving for more?

# 13:

## Obstacles

I T'S all very well having all these 'AHA' moments that I fully expect you're experiencing if you've been engaging with what I'm saying – especially if you've been answering the questions too. You are making fresh connections with who you're being right now and who you've shown up as in the past. Now, you are stepping more fully into your unique you-ness and learning to savour how you were designed to be different, which is a good thing. It's a worthy pursuit, but of course there are going to be a few lurking gremlins that show up and throw obstacles in your way, so let's look at a few of those before you head off into the wide blue yonder.

### Washington coffee stands aka instant gratification

When I first visited Washington State USA, I was mesmerised by all the coffee stands. It's hard to picture if you haven't seen them, but imagine that you can be in the back of beyond, without even a petrol station for miles around, and yet, you'll all of a sudden come upon something that resembles a garden shed, selling coffee, and possibly snacks, but mostly coffee. On my first trip out there, I was obsessed with them. It made me giggle at how we would be exploring the state and completely out of the way in a seemingly isolated spot far from civilisation, but we could still get (usually) good coffee!

One of the things I concede to liking about coffee stands is the instant gratification. I mean, what's not to love about being able to drive up and be equipped with caffeine without having to venture into the rain?

Don't we often want change to be like that too? I don't even mean for others. No, I bet you often have plenty of patience and understanding that they need time to learn and really get the hang of what we're asking.

No, I mean patience with yourself.

Many people I talk to are far more understanding, compassionate and into positive reinforcement when they're talking about their clients. When they're looking at themselves – yikes, things can become a lot more negative. Yet whether you're learning technical strategies or new mindset skills, you will pick some of them up quickly, and others will take time.

You don't need to be the queen of everything, because every mental skill you develop makes you more skilled than you were before, and just like your clients, some things are simply going to take time. And that's OK. It's good, in fact. Sometimes you'll hear something about how to tweak a specific aspect of your mental game and it'll be BOOM! Paradigm shift, one and done. More often, you – like your clients – will need practice, reinforcement and kindness.

I know getting what you want instantly is really nice, and we certainly live in a world that is really keen on instant gratification, but sometimes that drive-through instant gratification attitude hurts you when you're trying to learn for the bigger picture and long term!

I want to encourage you to slow down and resist the urge to want everything yesterday. Be kind to yourself in the process of learning and growing and trust that the things that take time do so for a good reason. Embrace the slow things as being lessons you need to learn deeply so that you are equipped for what lies ahead. Trust that where there is slowness, it is not to frustrate you, but to protect and strengthen you. To develop resilience and character, and so that your future will not be beyond your ability to stand strong in the midst of it.

The hidden trap in wanting everything NOW is that it gets you focused on the desired outcome, rather than the journey to your destination. It overlooks the value of the journey. I see this a lot in my clients and it will trip them up every time they succumb to it. So will you, so beware. What happens is that this instant gratification gremlin will get you so focused on the destination that you're not paying attention to what you're doing to get there, how you get there, or what you miss out on along the way. It's rather like being hell-bent on driving from Edinburgh to London and being so fixated on arriving in London that you are not paying attention to the road right in front of you. You're looking so far along the horizon for signs of Big Ben or Tower Bridge, that you're clipping other cars left right and centre, driving in the wrong gear, taking 'short cuts' through fields and having an absolute hissy fit when you come across traffic or roadworks. There's no pleasure in it and you'll never be satisfied until you get to London. Even then, it's been so hyped up and everything has been so dependent on your arrival there that it's likely to be a big disappointment! Even if it's not, it won't be long until the excitement wears off and exhaustion kicks in.

When instant gratification gets a hold of you, it can make things all about the short game. Taking your time and building towards something years down the line feels EXCRUCIATING.

The athletes who fall prey to this tend to focus on the potential win they could achieve in their next round, so even though they've an injury, that's getting worse, they'll step up to compete in a minor event anyway, even though they risk exacerbating the injury and making themselves unable to compete for weeks if not months. It's so tempting to sacrifice all the discipline they've worked on in training and just think about this event, even though it doesn't really matter. They sacrifice months of training – if not years – for the want of trusting the process and giving themselves time to heal so they're ready for the championships they ultimately want to be ready for. In my business clients, this instant gratification can show up in how they will take on clients that they know are not a good fit, in order to get the sale. Or they'll sell a course to someone today to get them into their world, without taking time to nurture the relationship and make sure that they really can serve this person with excellence. Both of these instant gratification responses can lead to short term wins but longer term losses. In the case of the ill-fitting client, this can be through stress of having to work with someone who is not a good fit, and then having to release them to a better fit and all the associated awkwardness that can involve. In the latter example, the lack of care to nurture clients and make sure that you're directing them to the best way to serve them with excellence can mean that a client leaves feeling that you couldn't help them, when in reality, if you'd resisted instant gratification and taken more time, you would have directed them to services which would have served them better.

We ALL love instant gratification. It is wonderful to get something we want, now. Yet if you can fight the urge to only think about the destination you want to get to, you can set milestones along the way. Think of them like scenic viewpoints along the road where you intentionally stop and look around. You might not be where you want to be, but you're not where you were. Sometimes it's not that the circumstances have changed, but that whilst you've been stuck in that 'traffic', *you* have changed.

## OVER TO YOU

- Where has the desire for instant gratification been stopping you from embarking on a longer-term project?
- If you find yourself struggling to invest long term in a bigger vision for yourself and your life, what holds you back?
- What does the 'gremlin' say to convince you that it's not worth your time or effort to embark on a bigger vision?
- Thinking of the people you were put here to serve, what are they going to lose out on if you only do work that gives you instant gratification?

### The comfort blanket of overwhelm

I wonder if you ever feel overwhelmed? It's a common problem I hear often from clients. This 'overwhelm' often happens when they have just decided or committed to going bigger, doing something new and stretching themselves to be, do or have more in their life. Here's the funny thing about overwhelm: overwhelm is your mind trying to keep you safe.

Let me give you a pretty blunt example from my own experience. It happened when I was in France one January on holiday, staying in a lodge in the depths of the Aquitaine countryside by a lake. The power went out on day two, so we spent most of the week without electricity. We had no lights, heat, wi-fi, or onsite way to keep our devices charged. It was freezing cold... and it was bliss.

In the midst of trying to keep warm and being in awe of our surroundings, I was thinking through the year, my clients, my Mastermind, the retreats I was planning, the new programmes I would be developing, my book, the new podcast...

At some point, I began to feel overwhelmed. It all felt so big, so much development that would be new and so many things that I didn't yet know would be successful. I believed I could do them all, but I didn't have the reassurance of past successes in all the new endeavours, yet.

As I was feeling overwhelmed, I really felt like God said, '"Overwhelmed" is a comfort blanket. You need to recognise it as such and not buy into it.'

WHOA.

I'm not shaming you if you're dealing with overwhelm – the feeling is real and it's horrible. But I do want to share with you what this spiritual two-by-four to the head taught me.

## The choice

What I realised was that whilst yes, my brain senses risk and wants to retreat under the duvet to what is familiar and what I KNOW I can succeed at... this is not what I am being called to do. This is not the way I help more people. It's not the way I model courage for others. It's not the way I get to experience the wild ride of living by faith.

I can have my comfort blanket of overwhelm and retreat into what my brain recognises as 'safe' and under control, OR I can have a word with my mind, recognise that it is trying to keep me safe by avoiding risk, but also realise that there is no magic or miracle to be experienced from under the safety of my comfort blanket.

The same is true for you.

## A non-negotiable

If you want to live life to the full, it *is* going to involve times when you feel uncomfortable, or downright out of your depth. You're not broken to feel that way. It's not weak to have fears. Everything new and big can feel scary.

If you're continuing to grow and change, it's not that fear leaves you, you just learn not to let it define or dictate your actions. It's always on the journey with you, in the car as it were. The difference is, you just don't let it drive.

Overwhelm is a way that your brain keeps you safe from trying new things or risking failure. It is often effective, it is common, and it does not have to win the day. You can choose to recognise it for what it is, honour that your brain is trying to keep you safe, and then decide what actions make most sense for you to take, however small, to move forward. Think about times in the past when you did hard things. When did you get through something, even though overwhelm tried to stop you? Maybe it was in school when you were preparing for an exam. As you think about this please note it does not matter what the outcome was in that case – that was then, this is now. The point is that you have faced overwhelm in the past and defeated it to get things done. That experience means that this is not your first rodeo, and that past experience may hold the keys to how you defeated overwhelm in the past and how you can overcome it again now.

## OVER TO YOU

- What risks does overwhelm keep you 'safe' from?
- What has it stopped you doing that would take you out of your comfort zone?
- How do you feel about that?
- What do you want to do in light of this awareness?

### The 'I' word

As you endeavour to become this fullest, feistiest living-by-faith version of yourself, don't be surprised if you are declared to be 'intimidating'. That is the 'I' word we're going to examine a little closer here.

According to Webster's, the word 'intimidating' means:

*'To make timid; make afraid; daunt'*[23]

If you're at all like me, you're perhaps already familiar with it. But let's look closer, at what this is really about.

The 'intimidating' person is declared so because of their effect on the other person in the dynamic. They're not self-describing as intimidating, well, not usually! Now whether that 'intimidating' person is TRYING to be intimidating is not even discussed, merely the effect they are perceived to have.

So here we have an example of someone who is having an emotional reaction to you (the so-called 'intimidating' person), and then trying to make you responsible for *their* emotional reaction to you. At this point let's just be clear that if you're trying to be intimidating, you'll want to have a wee word with yourself and ask what's going wrong that you're getting your jollies by using power that way. Assuming you're merely being you and having this thrown at you through no malevolent act or intent on your behalf, then you may want to consider whether 'intimidating' is actually your responsibility to hold, or not.

I picture it as a box, like a gift-wrapped present. Some boxes of responsibility are my responsibility to hold, some are yours. You may try to make me responsible for something that is yours to hold, but even though you try to get me to take responsibility and hold that box, it doesn't mean that it is mine to hold. Even if, for a while, I find myself holding it before I hand it back or set it down.

You are responsible for your conduct, but you are not responsible if someone finds your passion, your purpose, your desire to be or do more, to be uncomfortable to be around if they are not using their gifts or seeking to improve themselves. It is far easier to criticise someone else than it is to self-examine, especially when you know you've been dragging your feet. It is far easier to come up with excuses and self-righteous reasons why those people doing it are jerks, are wrong, or to justify why it's not the right time for you and that they should really back off.

If you've ever been told you're intimidating, consider why the person used that word to describe you. Were they trying to get you to play smaller? Were they trying to assuage their own guilt at not doing something with their own life? You'll notice that anyone who calls you intimidating is unlikely to be encouraging you to your best, wildest, most authentic self!

When someone uses that adjective to describe you, you have a choice: to conform and become more cookie-cutter, making yourself small enough to fit others' comfort level. OR you can lovingly hear what they feel, and then continue to become more fully who God put you here to be regardless. Just because someone has an opinion about you does not make you wrong. Take this latter path and it will be fresh, it will be challenging, it will be unique. It took far longer than I wish it had for me to wake up and realise that living my life authentically is MY job to work out, not my detractors. I can tell you that there is something truly liberating about not carrying others' emotional responsibility for what they feel when they interact with you.

This doesn't mean you're better than anyone else, it certainly doesn't mean you look down on anyone, and it doesn't absolve you of the responsibility to recognise and check your own attitudes and behaviour, but my goodness it's liberating to let go of taking responsibility for everyone else's reactions to you!

---

## OVER TO YOU

- If you've ever been called 'intimidating', what do you think it was about you that the person calling you that was reacting to?
- What strength in you might this description suggest you have?
- If we work on the premise that there are certain qualities God has to give you in order for you to be your best version of you in the world, why do you think you needed the qualities others feel are 'intimidating'?

---

OK so you get that being 'intimidating' is someone else's issue and their responsibility to work through, but there's still a temptation to self-censor. We all do it to an extent, and honestly? Sometimes that's a very good thing! Having a filter can certainly make life a lot less fractious. However, when it is fear shutting you down, then it's become something that we need to address head on.

## Self-censoring

*'Fearing people is a dangerous trap, but trusting the Lord means safety.'*[24]

Whether you have faith in God or not, the issue of dealing with others' opinions is a tough one, isn't it? We're so aware of what others will think, and worried about making fools of ourselves or falling foul of folks on social media, where our screw ups can go global and be seen by far bigger audiences than ever before. People who know nothing about you can form opinions on you and share those opinions, so daring to express any belief that dissents from the masses can be a scary prospect. In fact, you don't even need to be dissenting from the masses, just say something that someone doesn't like, and all manner of trolling can follow! Yikes.

In that context, who in their right mind would want to risk the nastiness, vitriol and potential harassment that could come from putting yourself out there?

It's not hard to see – whatever your worldview – that fearing people is a dangerous trap. It may promise short-term safety but even if it delivers that, it will still rob you of long-term rewards. It is so easy to become self-censoring and trying to self-police yourself to live within the perceived limits of social rules and norms, but if you truly understand that you have worth and purpose, then you know that there will be a time to speak up, regardless of the armchair grumblers and haters.

Whoever you were put on this earth to help needs you to use your voice, to be who you were created to be. To wield your influence wisely, no matter how small you may fear that influence is. Someone else needs you to show up fully, and be you, in the fullness and glory that the good Lord created you to have. Look back at some of the labels you were given in the past. What words no longer serve you? Which are like dead trees throwing shade on other plants that are healthy and capable of flourishing? Those unfruitful trees need to be removed. For the purposes of this analogy, they're restricting what could otherwise be thriving. You may have been told that you were 'too much' and of course you ARE for some people! Those are not your people, it's OK! You weren't put here to serve everyone. For goodness sake, we can't even all agree on what the best type of chocolate is, why on earth expect that everyone should appreciate you? The people who do resonate with you though, they'll get so much from being around you and learning from you... but only if you let them. Back to the chorus, sing along when you know the words, altogether now: 'You matter and you were designed to be different, so be uniquely you in all your glory!' Repeat to fade...

## Haters gonna hate

No matter what you do, people will judge you and have opinions on you. They may be wildly inaccurate, but that won't stop them having them!

It doesn't mean you have to pay attention to them. Just because someone has an opinion about you does not make their opinion right. Just because someone is offended by you does not automatically make them right.

Read those last two sentences again.

You cannot control what other people think of you, and only you can control how you choose to let their words and opinions on you affect you. Will they be a reminder to be accountable and look for anything truthful that you need to work on? Will they become something that helps you grow and communicate better? Or will they alter your course and make you live smaller?

I know that when I get out of alignment and fall into people pleasing or anything-for-a-quiet-life mode, it is frustrating as heck. I know it. I know when I'm playing small and I bet you know it too when you're doing the same. That's not to say that you do not need to take care for your personal safety when raising your head about the parapet on thorny issues. What I am referring to here is the distinction between genuine risk that must be managed, and where fear is just having a field day at your expense. It requires discernment to know the difference, but I bet that most of the time you know when your excuses are a steaming great pile of the smelly stuff, no matter how reasonable they sound, or how many people around you affirm them. You know that you're playing small and selling out on yourself, and you know that it is FEAR.

If you're spending your time trying to avoid upsetting anyone, you are expending a whole lot of energy you were never meant to spend! More than that, it's wasted time, when you could be making a difference. Argh! Don't throw your pearls before swine![25]

So how do you get over this and past it? Start putting one foot in front of the other. As you get clearer on who you are, whose you are and what you were put here to do, you recognise more that you are on a mission and that time is critical. Time is one resource you can't generate more of, so it needs to be treated as the precious commodity it is.

And then you start walking. One baby step at a time.

Recognise that people's opinions of you say as much about them as they do about you, and you can choose to bless and release them. You can choose to not take every single rant or response to you personally. You can choose to get curious about what caused that person to react in that manner, and if you're a person of faith, you will do a lot of praying!! I still need to get better at this, as I'm as good at self-righteous justification as the next person, all puffed up and defensive of my actions and motivations... what a waste of energy and demonstration of pride. Oof. But I'm #human like you. I'm still a work in progress, and God isn't finished with me yet either.

As you stop letting fear of others dictate your steps, you will see whole new paths opening up for you – whole new ways to interact with the people in your world that you can help. You'll find different relationships and perhaps even collaborations opening for you, in spaces that felt closed off before.

I'm not saying that it is easy, or something that you'll be fine with overnight, but I AM saying that you will notice a significant change as you step out and be who you were created to be.

You *will* repel the people whose cup of tea you are not, and that is GOOD. You *will* attract the people whose cup of tea you are, and that is where you can truly have a lasting impact. You do you, Boo – and let God take care of the rest.

## Personal development is an act of FAITH!

Before we move on, it would be naïve to pretend that this will all feel fun whilst you're in the messy part of untangling yourself from what has previously been holding you back. Waiting for your hard work to pay off is not the most fun part of the process, no matter how much you know to your bones that you're doing what you were made for and headed in the right direction.

Patience can be a right royal pain in the derrière, but in the waiting, good stuff happens. It's where growth happens, whether that's a child, a puppy or a plant. You KNOW this, and yet at some level it would be great if growth and progress could just hit fast forward and teleport you to the punchline, right? The stumbling block here is to grow impatient and think that delay means you're off track or never going to make it.

You don't get the fruit from a tree if you plant the seed one day and then bin it a week later because nothing has grown from it. Heck, it might be like the blueberry bush I bought, that didn't blossom, and a year later I found out was planted in the wrong blessed soil! No wonder it didn't thrive. Once I sorted that out, it was amazing! It took time to learn, trouble-shooting and patience to see the desired result. And it was worth it. Even if that bush had never yielded fruit, I still learned the lesson for future bushes.

Anticipation is the place of testing and refinement of your goal. It's a reaffirmation that you remain committed to doing what you need to do, and *being* who you need to become, in order to reach this next version of yourself and achieve what that iteration of you will be capable of. Good things come from the time of waiting, if we will only hang in there long enough, learn what we need to and trust the process.

## Anticipation is active

So, you find yourself in the in between. That's OK. As you have seen, it is *normal* for things to take time. Frustrating when we want everything yesterday, but normal nonetheless. While you anticipate what you want and dream of, I hope you've been grasping that waiting is not a stationary capacity, at least as I have been detailing it. The thing is that God is not going to give you something that will destroy you. You have free will so you can grab things before you're ready, but if you're listening to what I've been saying, it shouldn't surprise you that God will take His sweet time making sure that if He has given you a vision to build a multi-million dollar philanthropic business, for example, He will also intend to make sure that your character is ready to steward that business well and manage that income and the team you'll need in order to run it with excellence.

While you are in the season of anticipation, it's not a time to twiddle your thumbs. It's a time to prepare for what's coming and for who you will need to be so you can do what that season will require of you. You can't sit back and wait until the last moment to build either the skills or character that a new iteration of you requires, so part of the 'faith' involved in doing personal development work is trusting that the work you do now is valuable for the future that you cannot yet see. My dad has a whole lexicon of colloquialisms and one of his favourite sayings is that 'information is only as good as when you get it: it's no good, when you're up to your backside in alligators, thinking you should've drained the swamp'[26]. By the time you see the future arriving, you will have missed the opportunity to grow, so you have to take a leap of faith and get the mentoring, coaching or training you need BEFORE you see how the future is going to pan out. My client Laura Tsuk has a tip to share from our work together that you can use when the idea of being an active participant while waiting feels daunting.

### If she can, you can

Laura says 'My current favourite thing is the minimum viable action. As a teacher in dog training classes, I use it to help my students see even the smallest steps that they and their dogs are making towards their big goals. I really enjoy pointing out at the end of a six-week class session how those little steps each week have added up to big improvements.

For the business part of teaching it has helped me to make a syllabus for a class, make daily lesson plans and write homework. Most days, doing just the minimum viable action gets me started and I make more progress on whatever task I have chosen for that day but the joy is that even on the 'bad' days I can still count a victory in having done at least the minimum action! It allows me to

> see the big picture of a task but not be overwhelmed by
> the enormity of a project.'

These are just a few of the stumbling blocks that I commonly see clients falling into and they're certainly ones that my sorry behind has had to be dragged out of at times – and undoubtedly will fall into at times in future too, because let's not kid ourselves that any of us are going to wave a magic wand and somehow never make any more missteps. You and I are human, and if you look closely at the fine print on what it means to be human, it says 'screws up – a lot. Needs help – often'.

## OVER TO YOU

- Think about how you currently respond to each of these stumbling blocks we've touched on.
- How do you respond and what taught you to respond that way?
- When did you face similar challenges previously and respond in a different way? Look for the exceptions to the norm! The times when you did something different are important to pay attention to and investigate.
- How do you want to respond to these stumbling blocks in future?
- Who from your past knows that you can do that? Mentally recruit them and their perception of you to help you as you face them in future.
- If you're feeling brave, ask God who He says you are and how He wants you to face down these demons?

# 14:

## The mascara test:
## There's no one else coming

*But Moses again pleaded, 'Lord, please! Send anyone else.'*[27]

I want to walk you through a story. I heard a variation of it from a couple of my former coaches, and I've taken it and tweaked it into what I now call, 'the mascara test'.

As I walk you through this story, I want you to put yourself into it as much as possible, and don't second guess your responses. Just catch your thoughts and make note of them. Where details don't exactly fit your personality ('I never wear mascara'), don't get caught up in the precise elements, just run with it and make sure you're focused on the point, not the extraneous details. Now, are you sitting comfortably? Then I'll begin.

Imagine you are sitting on a picture-perfect beach. It's the sort of beach that would be used in an advert, it's that perfect. You're sitting there and you're by yourself, in complete serenity. All you can hear is the roll of the waves out in the most amazingly azure blue sea you can imagine, and you are just sitting there, enjoying the warmth of the sun on your skin. Everything feels idyllic.

Suddenly, out in the water, you see someone who is drowning. It's not like you see on TV, not all dramatic waving, but you can tell that they are DROWNING. The situation is urgent and as you realise this person needs help immediately, you look up and down the beach and realise that you're the only person there. What do you do?

There is only you, and this person does not have time for anyone else to come along. They need help NOW or it will be too late. What do you do?

Depending how you visualised this scene, perhaps there is a boat, or you have a surfboard or perhaps it is literally down to you to get into the water and save them. The water may not even be very deep. Maybe they got a cramp and you'd be able to save them without even needing to swim, but again, what do you do?

Do you worry about how you look scrambling to your feet and running to the water?

Do you worry that your wobbly bits are in full view and you're inelegantly swimming a doggy paddle stroke to get to this person? Do you stop to fix your mascara and make sure you're Instagram worthy before you go and save them?

I hope you don't, because that is not AT ALL what this person drowning cares about. What they care about is that you get your butt out there and rescue them. They're not going to give a flying fruitcake what you look like, how elegant your swimming style is, or how well made up you are, because if you don't get out there, there is no one else coming to save them. You are it.

There is another way that you may have looked at this story. Perhaps your gremlin wanted you to bemoan the fact that there was no one else there, or that there was only a rowing boat, and not a speed boat. Perhaps the gremlin was irritated that there was no one around to appreciate your efforts to save this person!

Maybe you find yourself eye rolling. I helped someone before, I ran out there, saved them and they didn't even thank me, or they thanked someone else and ignored me, or criticised me for how I saved them. Why should I help this person? They'll probably do the same, so what's the point in me getting all wet just to get criticised and used, again?

Note how those thoughts are all distractions from what the drowning person needs or cares about. That drowning person doesn't care what is impossible, they care that what IS possible is done. And that is where you come in.

## Step away from the mascara

The point of this is to consider how often you get caught up in how you look, the things you're insecure about, or what others will think about you. Oh, and note that when you worry about what others will think of you, you're not worrying that they're thinking how great you are. Ever notice that we're not worried they'll think we're too great, too gorgeous, too talented?! That little gremlin is happy for you to assume that anyone talking about you is saying NEGATIVE things.

With all that mental detritus going on, it's far too easy to be focused on those things and forget that you have purpose. There are people in your world who NEED you. Who need YOU. Not a hope of someone else stepping up and helping them in the future. They need you. Now. Today. You, with your tan lines, wobbly bits and tattered old bikini with the dodgy knicker elastic. The things you're worried about are not what they're paying attention to, because their problems are far bigger and more pressing than your insecurities.

It's super easy to wring your hands and bemoan all the things you don't have, all the skills you feel you lack, or the things that you're sure someone else could do better. But that Someone Else may be a myth. Even if they're not, THEY are not the person on the beach, in front of that drowning person. YOU are there, with the skills, abilities, talents, strengths, fallibilities and heart that you possess at this time. It's what YOU do that matters, not some possibly-imaginary-super-being that your fears dreamt up to try to stop you getting out there.

While you may have been doing the equivalent of putting on mascara and being concerned with that, there may be people right this minute who don't give a monkeys what you look like or how refined your brand/message/website/whatever is, they just need you to step up and show up to provide what they need.

## Quit looking at yourself

One thing I want you to see in light of the mascara test is that if you were sitting on that beach, afraid of not being able to help that person, afraid of how wobbly your thighs looked as you ran, or worrying about your mascara... you were focused on YOU. Not the person in need that you can help.

Don't feel bad, I'm not trying to shame you. The point is that this is one of the things fear does. It will turn your focus to you, to the exclusion of others, if you let it. It will present you with a thousand seemingly rational reasons why you can't or shouldn't get involved. It will tell you you're too busy anyway, or that the risk is too great. It might not do it if you can see someone's literal life is on the line, but when the stakes don't look that high, how often will it try to prevent you from doing what you can? Fear will give you all sorts of reasons to look busy but not be doing what you actually would be capable of, if you dared to get up off your butt and try.

Again, do not beat yourself up for this. Get mad at fear for being such a liar, for blowing smoke and obscuring the view, for making things so much more complicated than they need to be. Fear makes things seem so tough and makes out that you have to get them 'right' but that person who is drowning DOES NOT CARE about any of that.

You may be rolling your eyes as you read these past couple of sections, going 'I know this, you've said that already'. Good and yes, I have. I WANT you to be so familiar with these concepts that you're ready to eye roll. Then I want you to check yourself and ask if you're doing each of these things, or if your 'knowing' is only head knowledge. You may feel familiar with the concepts I'm raising with the mascara test, but are you living them? Get your notebook out because I have a few questions to nudge you into action with.

---

## OVER TO YOU

- In light of this mascara test, have a think: what 'mascara' have you been conned into worrying about instead of running headlong to help the people you can help?
- Who is right in front of you that needs what you have to offer?
- Where has fear been lying to you about what actually matters?
- What would you like to do differently?
- How does the mascara test help you cut through the noise?
- What will now change?

---

**15:**

## It's better than you think

W E'VE covered a lot of big ideas already and you may well have been facing down some baggage that has been weighing you down for decades, so before you leave this book for the next stage of your life's adventures, I want to finish off with a high-kicking cheerlead to encourage you and send you on your way. Pom poms at the ready, here I go.

### Infinitely more

*'Now all glory to God who is able, through His mighty power at work within us to accomplish INFINITELY MORE than we might ask or think.'*[28]

Your vision and God's vision may not always line up, and so I want to give you an example of being open to something so much better than you imagined.

What if it were true that there is a God and He so badly wants you to turn to Him and ask for His help and blessing? What if that God existed and was bursting to pour out treasures on you beyond what you can think up for yourself? I'm not talking about some genie that will give you piles of gold you can hoard to swim through like Scrooge McDuck, but who can give you peace when logically everyone would expect you to be losing the plot. Who has joy in spades for you, whether you're loaded or broke. A God who will do absolutely bonkers things for you, just because He knows that they'll make you laugh. If such a God existed, how would it change things for you? How might it feel if you could look up instead of having to try to find all the answers within yourself? What would be different if everything didn't depend on you to figure out, but you could hang out with this God and have Him give you ideas that you'd never have come up with on your own?

Again, I am not asking you to believe that, but to take a sidestep and look at how that might make you look at the world or your place in it differently?

Even if you are a Jesus-follower, the idea of having a God who is for you rather than waiting to nuke you can be a challenge. The idea of God loving you when you don't love yourself can sound so outrageous as to be offensive, and I have certainly been there. The idea of a God who is busting to forgive and make things right sounds nice in theory, but accepting that love when you're full of self-recrimination and can't forgive yourself, or are too proud to admit you've ever been wrong... it's easy not to live in the 'infinitely more' even if you are a believer! But what if?

## A view beyond your best hopes

If you choose to trust in the creator of the world, God, who made us unique and diverse and complex, then whatever you've been envisioning, buck up because it's nothing compared to what God may have in store. You may think you're dreaming big, but when you let God loose, you find that actually, you were thinking embarrassingly small!

I experienced this when I was living in Washington State, studying at graduate school, living from prayer to prayer to pay school fees and live. I told you early on about my crazy experience at my visa interview, but that wasn't even the half of it. That was merely a trailer for the main feature and all the wild things that would happen over the next three years. One of those was that, for my first year, I had rent-free accommodation with the incredible Marcia and Rick. I helped out where I could but it was rent-free, no bills, and a home with two wonderfully kind and wise people. Once that year was up, I needed more rent-free accommodation and I honestly did not know how I was going to keep paying for my tuition, let alone now find somewhere else to live. I had zero money for rent, so it absolutely needed to be rent-free – and that's such a common thing, right?!

I felt like I'd already had my miracle by getting the first rent-free home (and it *was* a home, I was with wonderful people and surrounded by similarly wonderful neighbours in that cul-de-sac), so the idea of getting more rent-free accommodation felt impossible. I sent out prayer letters, I was driving God crazy for an answer, I even went looking for a camper or caravan thinking that if I could rustle up the money for it, maybe that would be a way round it and would certainly be cheaper than an apartment. I was strung out.

## Acres of space with a killer view

Then God stepped in. What I had been asking for and what God gave me were two very different things. I couldn't have imagined what God would bring me. It was beyond what I would ever have thought to ask for, and yet, from the first moment I drove onto the property, I felt at home. It was a place of healing and the awesome couple whose place it was, Doug and Barb, are still two of the most important and cherished people in my world.

One of the people I had sent a prayer letter to – Michele – was someone I'd met at a dog agility training field on a freezing cold day. We were the only crazies there, and it actually started snowing as we chatted! Michele was a Christian and we went to the same trainer so we connected and got friendly. I went to *one* USDAA dog agility competition and at that, I met Michele's friend Bonnie for no more than two minutes as I was dashing between rings.

When I sent out my prayer letter, I wasn't even sure whether I should include Michele on the list, because I didn't know her that well and I didn't know if it was presumptuous and too forward to let her know my problem. Still, I decided to include her in the list to receive the desperate email I sent out.

Several days later, as I was out looking at fifth wheel trailers, I got a call from Michele that she might have a lead for me. It turns out that after receiving my email, she just so happened to be going to lunch with Bonnie and told her about my situation.

It just so happened that Bonnie was then meeting up with her best friend Barb...

Who just so happened to have a converted barn that they let out rent-free to needy souls...

And it just so happened that said barn had just become vacant...

And I found out years later that it just so happened that there was a breakdown in communications too, because Barb thought that Bonnie and I were close friends (remember: we'd literally only met for two minutes at that one competition) and it was on the basis of this assumed close friendship, that Barb offered me the opportunity to meet them, to see the barn and see if I could be their next tenant...

MY best plan was to buy a trailer. (I have NO idea where I'd have got the money for it nor where I'd have put it, I was just desperate and trying to be creative.)

GOD's plan was to provide somewhere I would not only be safe and secure, where I would not only be rent-free but where my hosts would refuse to even take money for bills, and where I would wake every morning and look out in awe on the Cascade mountains.

Hear me: I am NOT saying that when you trust God everything will be a wondrous haze of sunshine and unicorns. It won't. I AM saying that God is able and that His ideas are even better than yours. Whilst you'll also find some of your edges knocked off along the way for your ultimate good, there are times where God plain takes your breath away, and that is so that you learn more about trusting God for what lies ahead. God has no favourites, so if His plans were that amazing for me, there is no way that He wants less for you.

## OVER TO YOU

- What comes up for you when you read this catalogue of 'coincidences'? Does it make you smile? Do you feel cynical or want to explain it away?
- How does it feel in your body to imagine that there is a better plan for you than what you could even imagine? Does that attract or repel you? Why?

### You are the curator

My hope for you throughout this book is that you've begun to grasp more fully how valuable you are and how your specific make up is not accidental but by design. I hope you've caught the vision that you are not broken because you're not wired the same as everyone else. You were made to be unique and to help people from that uniqueness. The gifts, interests, passions God placed in your heart were put there because He knew they'd be a joy to you and through you they would also be a blessing to others. You are loved beyond measure and there never was, is not, nor ever will be anyone exactly like you.

As we wrap up our time here together, now it's over to you. *You* are ultimately the curator of what you've learned here. You decide what you do next and whether you implement what you've learned or let this book just be one more thing you've read and ticked off your list. I am cheering you on to implement every ounce of it that you've taken note of. There is limited point in reading more and more without actually *doing* anything with what you learn. So please make a plan for what you need to work on.

## Next right steps

I *know* how tempting it is to want to HAVE without the growth work of BEING, but that's just not how these things go. If you don't learn the lessons you need to learn at this stage, you'll find they come back around until you *do* learn them (often in increasingly tough guises!) and that learning comes before you are unleashed on the next 'level' that you desire. Take it as a vote of confidence that if you're constantly getting the sense that you're supposed to learn a specific lesson, you need it for where God wants to take you. You are facing that necessary lesson so that you can be equipped for what lies ahead.

'What got you here won't get you there' as Marshall Goldsmith put it. The personal development work that you need to do is crucial to getting where you want to go and having more of what you desire, whether that is impact, free time, money, health or whatever it is that is on your heart to step into.

## Life to the FULL

Are you ready to dig in and take the time, be patient, and do the deep work of becoming this next iteration of you who embraces a bigger vision for her future?

If so, let's work together to achieve that.

Working with me is not for those who are only thinking about changing or doing something more with their life. This is for you if you are determined to understand your worth and purpose, you want to stop striving and work at an un-hustled, God-designed pace in a way that is an absolute blast for you.

If this is you, go to **www.drkathrine.com** where you will find links to my Mastermind, 1:1s, retreats and courses as well as my podcast, blog and free resources. I look forward to helping you take your notes and plans from this book and bringing them to life! Let's go!

# Postscript: An invitation

**H**AVING waxed lyrical from my faith perspective throughout this book, it would now be downright weird if I didn't give you an opportunity to experience that for yourself, if you want to, of course. I wouldn't take the time and effort to write this for you if I hadn't experienced life both with and without God's input and seen the difference letting Jesus into my world has made. I also walked away from my faith for years to do things my own way, and well, let's just say that I came back because it came to my attention that my *sans-Jesus* existence was a hot mess in comparison.

I DO NOT want to invite you to dead religion or to turning up on Sunday to be seen and be ticked as present on some heavenly attendance sheet. I have no desire to invite you to smells and bells and walking around like you've been baptised in lemon juice. Nope. I also have no desire to invite you to something that manipulates the name and character of Christ for financial or political gain.

I do want to share with you that I fervently believe that God loves the stink out of you and really wants to walk with you through each day. As the one who made you and purposed you, I know that He has insights that He'd love to share with you, and there are definitely times where He'd love to have you ask for help and advice.

You have free will and God is never going to contradict that, so if you don't want a relationship with Him, He's certainly not going to force your hand. He'll honour that and you'll have sole right and responsibility for what comes next.

If you want to experience what life looks like with Jesus on board, it's dead easy. You've just got to ask. Admit you're not perfect, admit you need help, invite Him into your world to be CEO of your life and saviour of your eternal spirit.

Look, this isn't about limiting you. It's about reconnecting you with God, and giving you a fresh family to do life with. It's about life to the FULL (John 10:10). If you've come this far and you want to jump in with Jesus, here's just a wee example of a prayer you could pray, a chat you could have with Him to invite Him into your life.

*God, I know you created me and have a purpose for my life. I know you want a relationship with me and we haven't had that up to now. God, you are perfect and I am not perfect, I've messed up along the way, I've done wrong things, please forgive me and make things right between us. Jesus, I want you to come into my life. I want you to be my Lord and Saviour and guide my life. I want to trust you. Amen.*

If you've invited Jesus into your life, please let me know!

Contact me via **www.drkathrine.com** so I can send you some resources and celebrate with you!

# Notes

## Introduction

### Chapter 1

**1.** One irritating thing about the term 'impact' is that it is often used in ways that suggest correlation with money earned or number of clients you have worked with. Respectfully, I disagree. Of course you hope that working with someone is impactful but since your clients' results are at least 50 percent down to them, and that impact is NOT limited to money-making activities, I invite you to think more ambitiously about the idea of you having impact. You matter, regardless of your productivity, regardless of your bank balance.

## Part 1

### Chapter 2

**2.** Proverbs 18:21a *New International Version (NIV)* Bible.
**3.** Throughout this book, some names have been changed for privacy reasons.
**4.** Proverbs 18:21 in *The Message* translation of the Bible: 'Words kill, words give life; they're either poison or fruit – you choose.'

### Chapter 3

**5.** John 10:10 *New Century Version (NCV)*

**6.** Check out Ephesians 6:12 for more on this. *The Amplified Bible* says it this way: 'For our struggle is not against flesh and blood [contending only with physical opponents], but against the rulers, against the powers, against the world forces of this [present] darkness, against the spiritual *forces* of wickedness in the heavenly (supernatural) *places*'.

Chapter 4

**7.** C S Lewis, *The Lion, the Witch and the Wardrobe*, (2009). London: HarperCollins Publisers Ltd, p89.

Part 2

Chapter 5

**8.** Collins English Dictionary
**9.** De Becker, G (1997). *The gift of fear: Survival signals that protect us from violence*. London: Bloomsbury Publishing PLC, 65.
**10.** Reby, D, Levréro, F, Gustafsson, E et al. Sex stereotypes influence adults' perception of babies' cries. *BMC Psychol 4*, 19 (2016). https://doi.org/10.1186/s40359-016-0123-6
**11.** From the film version of *Shirley Valentine* by Willy Russell.
**12.** It was the early 90s! Technology meant something quite different to what you'd expect it to mean now!

Chapter 6

**13.** Okimoto T G, Brescoll V L, The Price of Power: Power Seeking and Backlash Against Female Politicians. *Personality and Social Psychology Bulletin*, 2010; 36(7):923–936. doi:10.1177/0146167210371949
**14.** Bennett, Jessica, "How Not to Be 'Manterrupted' in Meetings", *Time*, 20th January, 2015, https://time.com/3666135/sheryl-sandberg-talking-while-female-manterruptions/

**15.** Criado Perez, C (2019). *Invisible women: Exposing data bias in a world designed for men*. London: Chatto & Windus

**16.** According to Payscale.com

**17.** https://www.citation.co.uk/news/hr-and-employment-law/sex-discrimination-during-interviews/

**18.** https://www.livingwage.org.uk/news/news-women-continue-be-hit-hardest-low-wages-uk

## Part 3

### Chapter 7

**19.** Psalm 121: 1–2 *New Revised Standard Version (NRSV)*

### Chapter 8

**20.** Jesus speaking in Matthew 11:28–30 *The Message* translation of the Bible.

### Chapter 9

**21.** Look them up: https://www.irregularchoice.com

### Chapter 12

**22.** GCSEs are qualifications that 16-year-olds take in UK. You take them in chosen subjects and your grades are used to determine whether you can continue to A-levels, which are the highest qualification that you can achieve in secondary/high school. Passing grades at English and maths may also be specified on job applications.

### Chapter 13

**23.** Webster's *New World College Dictionary*, 4th Edition. Copyright © 2010 by Houghton Mifflin Harcourt. All

**24.** Proverbs 29:25 *New Living Translation (NLT)*

**25.** Matthew 7:6b. Yes, that is a wisdom direct from the Bible.

**26.** Before you tell me of any inaccuracies in the logics of this saying, don't get too literal… and remember that we have neither swamps nor alligators in Northern Ireland, so this is just a phrase he uses to make a point!

## Chapter 14

**27.** Exodus 4:13 *New Living Translation (NLT)*

## Chapter 15

**28.** Ephesians 3:20 *New Living Translation (NLT)*, emphases mine.

# Acknowledgements

NO book happens without a team who support you, believe in you, critique drafts, edit, and cheerlead you along the way. I have more people to express gratitude to than I have words for, but since I can already hear the orchestra gearing up to play me off stage, here are the main actors who helped me get this book out into the world for you to read.

When I decided to write a book, it was Jessica Killingley who taught me where to even start. Jessica, I am so grateful for your sweary expertise and generosity with your time. You showed me I could do this and it is in no small part your fault/credit that this book is only the first of multiple. Isabelle Knight, your insights into all things publicity and brand story have taken my vision and crystallised it. You're a joy to work with and make it all so much easier than I'd hoped. Erin Chamberlain, thank you for being my editor and project manager. Having you guiding me on the moving parts of publishing has been a truly fun experience which I am profoundly grateful for. Every book worth its salt has beta readers and mine are powerhouses in their own right: Gillian Barrett, Cortney Browning, Nandi Dossou, Sian Gilmartin, Susan Fleming, Paige Killian, Lauren Malone, Nika Maples, Angela Quinteros and Monica Speight. I am forever grateful for your time, rich feedback and enthusiasm for this book.

One of the biggest blessings God ever gave me is my sister, Jenny, who is my right-hand woman and has been for the last decade. Thank you Jenny for being my sounding board, the woman who gets things done, and the one who makes me laugh till my ribs hurt. Bringing you on board was one of the best business decisions I have ever made and I love beyond words that we get to do this work together!

At the risk of sounding like that person on the radio who uses their shout-out time to thank everyone they've ever met, I want to thank my clients past and present. Getting a front row seat to your epiphanies and transformed lives never gets old. Thank you for letting me into your world and keeping me posted over the years with your continued successes. I still read and cherish every one.

Beth and Scarlet, so much of my fire to do this work in the way that I do is to leave this world a little better for both of you. I love you both to pieces and am fiercely proud of the women you are and are becoming.

Finally, Ben my darlin', my team mate in life, supplier of cups of tea, glasses of wine when tea is not sufficient, and the maker of sublime meals. Your steadfast love and unwavering support have carried me through many a writer's and entrepreneurial low point, and having you to celebrate the highs with makes them all the sweeter. I'm so grateful God gave me you to do life alongside, to laugh till we cry, and be at the beck and call of Blitz with!

# Index

# About the author

DR Kathrine McAleese is a former queen of burnout, personal development and business coach, a dog lover and a purposeful follower of the Christian faith. Combining her faith with her straight talking, 'fireside chat' humour and view of life, Dr Kathrine is adept at allowing her readers to create time and space for themselves, to view their lives, desires and success from an empowering standpoint of self-acceptance, combined with unapologetic self-knowledge and faith, which ultimately leads to an un-hustled, rewarding and enriching, God-designed life.

To access the resources that accompany this book, go to: www.drkathrine.com/enough-resources

Find out more about how you can work with Dr Kathrine at www.drkathrine.com

CPSIA information can be obtained
at www.ICGtesting.com
Printed in the USA
LVHW111548111222
735011LV00006B/712

9 781739 167509